Reflections With My Reflection

CLARA FLEMING

So You Can Write Publications, LLC

PO Box 80736

Milwaukee, WI 53208

www.sycwp.com

ISBN-13: 9781734757026

Cover design by: www.sycwp.com

Printed in the United States of America

TABLE OF CONTENTS

Acknowledgements

As with every accomplishment in my life, I must first thank my higher power, who I choose to call God. Without God in my life I wouldn't have made it to this point, nor could I become the person I am destined to become.

I thank my children, Rashidah and Ajamou, who have loved and respected me, even with what they have known. They are true examples of loving me unconditionally. Now that they know the sides of me that are revealed in these pages, their love and respect has increased. They've encouraged and supported me. When my fear of judgment made me want to abandon this project, they wouldn't let me.

Shout out to Dr. Katina Fuller-Scott. She supported me in the days of this project when I didn't know how to do it; I only knew that it had to be done. She was my cheerleader and prayer partner all in one. That woman of God is a constant force.

Brenda Sinclair, my ride or die, my partner in crime. She has spent endless hours listening to me and provided what I needed, including friendship and food. She is the one person who may love this project more than me.

Justin Horne is the person who convinced me to finally see this project through. What my friend told me will stay between us, but the world will see the results of those conversations. I thank him for seeing the value in what I wanted to ignore.

Morgan Gathings, my photographer. What can I say? She is phenomenal as a creative spirit and as a woman. Getting to know more of her has been a pleasure.

Joe Heru Cook wrote a poem that we both knew had to be a part of this project. He has a story of his own and I hope one day he tells it. I know it will change lives.

To my editor and inspiration, Tia Love, who is the founder of Penned By Love and an accomplished writer herself. I could not, would not, have done this without her support and expertise. My bonus daughter has become what I want to be and proven to me that the time is now.

To the countless others who supported me, believed in me, and listened to me, you know who you are, and I thank you all.

Foreword

This is my first book and it has taken decades, a life worth of decades to write. It may not be written the way most books are written. I refer to my reflection as you, and us. All of us are complicated creatures. We are multifaceted and if we don't reflect with our reflections we dim the brightness within us. I put my life on paper for two main reasons. The first is to show that transformation is possible. We don't have to be today who we were yesterday, or who we may be tomorrow. The second reason is to promote healing. Disease left untreated will not heal itself.

The poem included by Joe Heru Cook speaks to how I see myself and womanhood in general. I've allowed myself to become rooted in truth and because of that I've grown towards the sky. I remain grounded in my truth. The poem titled Reflection of Me was written years ago when I was trying to deal with that part of my life. Little did I know that this piece would become the theme of a book.

Let us not despise the day of small beginnings. My hope is that everyone who reads this book will learn about my life, but furthermore that they learn about their own life. I hope you get the courage to reflect with your own reflection and be brave enough to let your reflection speak back.

I leave you with one request – ask yourself if you had to tell your entire life story to the world, what would you leave out and why?

I wish you bountiful blessings,

Clara F.

Reflections

Rooted in Womanhood
By Joe Heru Cook

She stood statuesque
naked to the flesh
hands raised towards the sky
rooted and reaching.
I walked in on her
A private moment.
"Oh, excuse me."
I turn to leave
"No, you can stay.
I'm a tree today.
Rooted and reaching towards the sky.
I have layers to me
Beneath this brown skin
There are layers that tell my story
Like the rings underneath the brown bark of a tree.
I'm layered with more than what the eye could ever see."
I think silently.
Like the maple tree,
She's tough enough to become furniture
Yet sugary sweet.
She spoke.
"Layers, rings, women are like trees,"
She proclaims, full of enthusiasm
As if she just had an awe-ha moment and had to tell
somebody.
I look at her naked body with awe
Curiosity and imagining.
Sexy, yes
But right now, sex has to digress.

As her flesh becomes bark
And her body becomes the visual art.
She continues,
"You won't believe what I've been through,
Summer, spring, fall, and winter too.
Weathering the storm and standing tall
Like phenomenal women do."
Her flesh becomes bark.
Her limbs become branches.
Her words become leaves, oxygenating me.
I breathe.
I rub my eyes.
I blink a few times.
Her toes, her legs, her thighs
Become a tree stump.
She transforms before my eyes,
Tree-like, rooted and reaching toward the sky.

Reflection of Me

In my constant nightmare, she dropped out of school and then out of life. She made money on the block to get the rock. She'd be a millionaire had she invested in bonds and stocks. Why am I dreaming this craziness? Did I stay up too long or was it something I ate? I wake up sweating with a fast heartbeat. I close my eyes again and I try to sleep. I hear the sound of her heels going click clack as she walks the street another hoe trying to pick up her next trick. She has no feelings about picking up some woman's husband and committing a paid for sin. The only time she feels anything at all is when the needle goes in. Again, I'm awake, wondering who the child of God could be and why her existence is being relived by an outsider like me. I drift off again, afraid to close my eyes. When I do, I see man after man between her thighs. I see her in a parked car. I hear the zipper go down and see a hand on the back of her head. She thinks about the next hit and she gags but doesn't spit. She wishes she was dead. He continues to push down her head. What the hell is this dream about? I'm awake now, but I still hear her shout into the payphone as she calls her mother and says all is really well, and those stories are lies made up by her father and brother. She hangs up the phone and catches a cab back to the Motel 6. She cooks the dope and knows getting more means sucking more nasty dicks, getting with freaky tricks. She hates herself. I hate her too, because in my dreams, I live her life, too. She runs away from the pimp when he beats her ass and hides between buildings on a urine-soaked concrete slab. What the hell is wrong. I'm starting to regret the invasion of this crazy bitch. If her stupid ass would have kept half the money she made, no doubt she'd be more than rich. I hear the gun go click. I saw him put a bullet in the chamber. He points the gun at her head while he repeatedly rapes her. She feels nothing, not even anger. He laughs and throws her clothes down at her feet. She dresses and he tells her to get out on some anonymous street. I feel the whelp rise up from the blow of the wire hanger. Again, she feels nothing. Not even anger. I want to save her and give her hope, but all she wants anyone to give her is another hit of dope. I beg this unknown sister of mine to run away. She says he always finds me, no matter where I try to stay. The next thing I know, in the blink of an eye, I see her in jail and hear her childlike cry. I can't tell if she is crying because she is locked up or she is in desperate need of getting high. In every scene I see her in, I notice she is getting so thin. I hear her say 200 dollars an hour. That seems like a cheap price to give up your power. I say out loud, I want to help you. I want to be your friend. She says there are no friends in this life. I'm just waiting for my life to end. If you really want to be my friend, there is no need to tell me your name. If you want to be my friend, I'm having trouble getting a hit, help me find a usable vein. I go to the bathroom. I throw up and sit on the floor and cry. There seems to be nothing I can do to help her than to let her slowly die. She makes ridiculous amounts of cash money every day, but she has nothing to show. Turning tricks, being pimped, and getting high is all she really knows. I get up from the floor and look in the mirror. I see the face of the strung-out whore. She has the same face as me. All this time I thought I was dreaming of seeing an anonymous face. It turns out that the woman I tried to forget had followed me to this place. At first I didn't know who this young girl could be. But it turns out that I'm remembering and embracing the fact that she is me.

Part One

Greetings From the Glass Gateway

I stepped from the stinging yet pleasurable hot shower. I knew that once I wiped the layers of steam from the full-length mirror that I would be exposed not only in my nakedness, but in my naked truths and vulnerabilities. I took my time deciding which part of the hidden reflection to uncover first. I opted to start at the top and work my way down, although no way to completely expose my reflection seemed comfortable to me.

Slowly my hand disrupted the condensation that revealed my face, thinning hair, and what I have been told are my hypnotic, spell-casting eyes. Facing the face that looks at me from the mirror has never been a pleasant experience for me. I told people for years, I told myself for years that I didn't wear makeup because I was a natural beauty who didn't need it. The lie came so easily that over time, I myself believed it.

When I could no longer hold the poisonous taste of that lie inside me, I threw it up and replaced it with the truth. I didn't wear makeup because I couldn't stand to look at myself long enough in the mirror to put on anything more than cocoa butter, lip gloss, or eye drops during my smoking phase, which came after my speed ball phase.

I stared at the eyes that stared at me and looked beyond their unique, intense color. More than fifty years of life was reflected back at me. It was a life I thought would end before twenty-five. Yet miraculously, more than twice that time had passed, and I was still here, because of the grace of God who for the most part saw more value in my life than I did.

New life coming into the world has been witnessed by my eyes. I saw the c-section birth of my daughter and son through those eyes. There were many more babies I saw come into this world including babies born in the village family. Almost sixteen years at the hospital gave me the privilege to consistently witness that miracle of life. I've also been blessed to witness the other part of that miracle, death.

The fact that I got a second chance at life is what made me go into health care. My life was spared, and I wanted to work with those who wouldn't be able to say that. So, I worked in home hospice and spent time with many people who took their last inhale of air before exhaling their life. I got skilled at knowing when life was leaving, probably because I'd seen my own come close so many times that I could see death hovering to take the life of one who couldn't choose to fight any longer.

My eyes used to be the eyes of an eagle. I could thread a needle with just one or two attempts and no glasses. I used to be able to spot the thinnest vein and shoot up the cocaine and heroin concoction that I needed and couldn't afford to waste with a blown shot. When I could no longer find usable veins in my arms, hands or feet, I was forced to shoot up in my jugular vein. I hated that most because I had to look in the mirror, and when I did, I wanted to vomit up the self-hatred that boiled in my belly.

I learned only once I got tired of sharing my dope, paying people to often hit me, paying the price of the package and feeling like a bigger fool than I already felt in the first place for wanting to go last. The man I was with when I started using, the man I thought I loved always made me wait for him to go first. A minute is an hour to a dope fiend. I knew better than to ask to go first but on the rare occasions that I did, one of my pretty golden-brown eyes would become a sad painful portrait in a frame of black, blue, and purple. A collage of "how dare you disrespect me" and "what makes you think you're above me, Bitch." I was sure that he loved me, but not as much as he loved the dope. I couldn't be too mad about that because I didn't love me as much as I loved the dope either.

My eyes replay the scenes of the open-handed slaps that I couldn't defend myself from for fear of bringing on a worse punishment for some minor infraction. I saw the smiles of those who said they loved me. No coincidence, I suppose that it was occasionally the same people in both scenes.

I look farther into my eyes and I relive the birth of my two beautiful grandbabies who call me Grandma. Even though I share DNA with only one, I share my heart with both. I smile because my daughter is pregnant now and I can't wait for my firstborn to give birth. I looked deeper into my eyes' memory and see the only sibling I had, my brother, being lowered into the ground because he lost his fight with liver cancer. Or, maybe he didn't lose, but instead surrendered and threw in the white flag. Either way, cancer can no longer touch him. The sad part for me is neither can I. He wasn't even fifty.

I see myself holding the arm of our father that day, a God-fearing man who believed he'd see his only son again one day. I took some comfort in that because at the time of my brother's death, our dad was in his mid-80s, so I figured he knew what he was talking about. Mama didn't get to her son's funeral. She swore after burying her own mother that she wouldn't attend another funeral except her own, and she stayed true to that.

Though I now require glasses to see some things, my eyes, rare in color, often with dark circles beneath them, have served me well. They have made men and women become tongue-tied feel bashful, and they have comforted babies. They have caused some to flee, claiming that they could see Satan's face when looking at my eyes. I allow my eyes to travel to the top of my head.

A woman's hair is her crowning glory. If this is true, I wear four crowns because of the four different types of hair on my head. One is sprinkled with gray. One is thinning, but still visible. One is baby fine, fine and naturally curly while the last is stubborn like me, and wants to do its own thing. It is kind of straight, kind of curly, following no particular pattern, again, like me. My hair endured the pressing comb every week as a girl. Sometimes I'd sit in the kitchen while Mama or Grandma did my hair. Other times, I'd sit in somebody else's kitchen to get my kitchen straightened out.

Although I'm not in favor of burning hair to death, I do mourn the hair of my youth. My crowning glory has gone from permed to afro, to honey blonde locs, and now this. This tuft of hair that makes me resemble my mother and everyday I run my fingers through it, which doesn't take long mind you, and I wonder what's next. What crown will be the next to sit on top of my head?

Now that I can look at myself and not be repulsed by the face that looks back, I realize that I can't afford to lose anymore hair, and I try sometimes to count the grays. I used to wish them away, but I need every hair I can get. Plus, those stubborn gray hairs are part of the reason my daughter says that I look like my mother when I have my little afro, especially when I put my glasses on. I've almost accepted that when it comes to hair, it is what it is. Besides, the gray is beginning to give me the salt and pepper look about the temples which, if I do say so myself, is rather suitable for a woman as distinguished as myself.

The man that I share just a piece of myself with actually likes my hair and whatever I do to it, or for that matter, whatever it does to itself. He has love for me, so I guess to him it doesn't matter. He sees beyond that. I think to myself; wouldn't it be nice if we could all see each other below the surface?

I am rubbing my hair, remembering a time when it was a big issue in a relationship. A man I had known for years as a friend, decided to step to me and take the relationship further than friends with benefits. We dated exclusively for a while. During the years he'd known me, he saw me in various hairstyles. At the start of our relationship, my hair was braided. Things were going fine but after some time he said, "we need to talk."

We all freeze up at those words because it usually means something is coming that may be a bit hard to take, good or bad, one way or another. I was totally not prepared for the conversation. He told me that my hairstyle wasn't working for him. He felt that it wasn't as feminine as he preferred. He wanted me to take my braids down and perm my hair so it would give off a softer look that would better match the image he wanted his woman to have.

I wanted to cuss his ass out big time, but I didn't. First opportunity I got, I ran to the beauty shop to get the braids out and put the chemicals in. I allowed him to dictate my look, and make me feel less than a woman. I kept my mouth shut and did what made him comfortable, all at my own expense. That story gets even more tragic because a short time later, again, he wanted to "talk." This time he told me that the relationship wasn't really working for him. He didn't think I was the type of woman he should be with and he wanted us to go back to being friends or whatever we were before our relationship.

I remember another incident involving my hair that affected my self-esteem. About twenty-five years ago, I found a moment to take myself for a walk in the park. Those moments were rare with caring for two small children and working two jobs at the time. As I walked along the path approaching a bench to sit, a random man walked towards me from the opposite direction, I took a chance and sat and just as I figured he would, the man sat too. He struck up a conversation with limited skills. He had no game and I would know because game recognizes game.

Eventually, like I knew he would, he asked if I had a man or if I was married. He had the nerve, with his ugly behind, to tell me that if I put on a little makeup and fixed my hair that I could easily get a man, maybe even a husband. I wanted to cuss him out too, but I had no words to describe what I thought. So, instead, I got up, feeling a sudden burning in my throat and eyes that threatened the onset of tears. I walked fast and then faster towards my car as he followed, talking about, "I didn't mean no harm. Wait a minute miss lady, you don't look that bad. I didn't mean to say it like that."

Finally he stopped following me. I turned around and saw him walk in the opposite direction and then I jumped in my car. I remember I couldn't even drive away. I just sat there for a few minutes and cried, thinking that once again, a man had knocked me to my knees and this time he didn't pay. I found myself looking in the mirror in the car. I remember thinking, am I bad looking? Isn't bad a relative term? Who can say what's bad? Was my hair broken like it needed fixing?

My stomach hurt as I relived that memory of allowing the words of a stranger to make me feel broken and ugly. I remember that my own mother used to offer to send money every week to get my hair fixed. It made me think about the generational damage we as mothers sometimes do to our daughters by telling them in subtle ways that they are not good enough just as they are. *Fix your hair, you need a man to complete you, you have to go to college, put a little makeup on, fix yourself up.* There is that word 'fix' again. Don't we realize the power of words? *Keep your husband happy. What do you mean you don't want children?* I sat in my car that day thinking that I want my little girl to be happy and whole the way she is, on her own platform living her truth.

I'd focused on my hair long enough and now examined the skin on my face. Not yet showing the years like it could have, especially considering everything I've been through. But I know that Black women, for the most part, age gracefully, especially if we take care of ourselves, which later in my life I had started to do. I didn't think I was bad looking.

There is another word that we take on sometimes from men, or those who look like us or even those who are us. *Bad.* Let me work harder to change how I speak about myself. Besides aren't looks more about preference. Shit, I've been to hell and back and I've had a roundtrip ticket several times. I'm not one to brag, not often anyway, but I don't look like what I've been through. Thank God for that.

Time has marked the passage of my life's years by anointing my face with moles from my father and the rest of his family. Based on my childhood memory, my father inherited them from his father, who used to sit on the porch in the evening in an old rusty metal rocking chair or porch swing and eat day-old cornbread with buttermilk. He would crumble the cornbread in the buttermilk to create the daily delicacy that he craved. I always thought it was strange that the cornbread had to be old. I asked my auntie one time why Granddaddy only used old cornbread when she made fresh and new bread every day. She told me that he didn't mind that for supper, but everything had a place and the place for day-old cornbread was in his bowl of buttermilk.

As a child I didn't understand that, but now I do. There are some days that I feel old, or at least middle-aged, and it comforts me to know that like the day-old cornbread, I have a purpose and I'm still useful. I'm useful to the world and to God. According to the bible, I can be like the ass mentioned in chapter twenty-two of the Book of Numbers. If God could use the ass and give it a voice to deliver a message, surely he could do the same for me.

There are messages everywhere, we just have to be aware. I think of my grandfather whenever I make cornbread or look at the moles on my face. Then I smile. I smile even harder when I realize that my father who I've most often called by his first and middle name has the same face moles as his dad and me. Someone asked me once would I ever consider having them removed. Of course not. Why would I want to have the very thing removed that makes me look exactly like where I come from? That would be a denial of my family. I can't even remember who asked me that but how insensitive that we are more caught up in looks than legacy.

My parents divorced when I was six, which means my little brother was about four. Our father remained on the outer edge of our life after that. But we spent weekends with him while he lived in the same city. Once he moved back south, where he was from, we would go down and spend time in the summer with him. Even though I know that we were not close as most would define it, there were a couple of times in my life that he was there to keep the bottom of my life from breaking beneath me.

The first time I remember feeling like that was at fifteen. I had just been released from the psych ward after a failed suicide attempt, which was really just a phone call for help with an attempt. Either way, I could not face the disappointment that radiated from Mama, and I needed a place to go. So, I asked both parents if I could stay with Daddy down south for a while. They agreed. I never moved back home and in the years that followed, I may have spent five nights at Mama's house, and that's being generous. It was probably less.

Within a few months of leaving Minnesota and moving to Charleston, South Carolina, I was turned onto what was called the life, but it should have been called death since that was what it really offered. I still maintain that to this day, my choices to get involved in drugs, prostitution or even to drop out of school was not the fault of either of my parents. They were just that. My choices.

The older I get, the more I realize the value in taking responsibility for my own choices. I don't even know who I'm telling that to. I hear my voice and it dawns on me that I'm talking out loud, maybe to the partial reflection I see, maybe to myself. I know we are one, but we are also separate. Maybe I'm talking out loud to you God. I often do. Sometimes my prayers seem more meaningful when I say them out loud. If I can hear me, then I know you can hear me, Lord and I'm feeling some things today. But I need to do this my way and I appreciate you giving me that ability.

Anyway, as I'm looking at that face looking at me, I'm transported back to that time when it all started to go wrong. Actually it went wrong before that and this was the time it went from wrong to terribly wrong. But my father, who knew me but didn't know me, took me in, no judgment just love, the unconditional kind. The second time he was there to save me, I decided I was really done with my fast life, or rather my slow death.

I don't know if my words or their sequence will make sense to anyone else, but they do to me, and today I can't stay mute or whisper them, or worse, swallow them, anymore. The taste makes me nauseous when they go down. No, today is the day to expel them loudly, even if no one hears them but God and me.

Remembrance can be good for the soul when followed by acceptance.

Part Two

The Beginning of the End

I was twenty-two when I was done for the last time. I was done with the drugs, the sex for money, the things I wouldn't even define as sex, the hotels for homes, the abuse, and the continuous downward spiral of my self-esteem. I was done with the whole ball of bullshit. This time I meant it. I called my father and asked him to come get me. He knew what I did but I always tried to keep it away from him as much as possible. My father came with a couple of friends to rescue me. I ran from the bushes where I hid when I saw the car pull up and I jumped in.

The day I made the final "I'm done this time" decision, it was raining. It had rained all day and *he* was getting out, so I took the day off to prepare. I copped the dope, had the liquor, and cancelled all business of a sexual nature. It was just going to be us. I came in from the rain and laid the umbrella against the old radiator that provided heat to the dampness.

Before he could come home, he had to stop at the local hangout and let everyone know he was back. It was there that our life unraveled, yet again. He checked in with the other players in the game and haters that they were, they couldn't wait to tell him what I'd done to disgrace him in his absence. It didn't matter that I'd kept business going, stacked up paper, picked up new tricks, kept plenty of money on his books or didn't run off when I had the chance. What mattered was the disgrace that he now had to live with.

Yes, they told him of the rule I broke. God, why did I do it? I knew better but was only thinking of my desire at the moment, not the consequences of my actions. They told him how I'd gone to another pimp that he knew well and gave him money to cop my dope. I was really, really busy that day laying on my back and getting on my knees. I knew Slim was going to cop, so I paid for his package.

I broke rule number one in the life – trust no one and anyone you dare to trust should only be trusted in your line of sight. So they told him and teased him in good fun but also in a mocking way. He came in the door and asked me if it was true. Was what true, I said, sitting on the side of the bed wrapped in only a sheet figuring that was less to take off once the "get-high" sex started.

Why did I do it, he asked. I was waiting for him to tell me how pleased he was with me for holding things down while he was locked up, and here he was questioning me about something that still hadn't clicked in my head. Once he told me he had been to the diner, the look of fear that crossed my face told him that I knew exactly what unforgivable sin I had committed.

It wasn't worth discussing. There was nothing I could say. I had no defense at all, at least none that was going to be acceptable to my judge, jury, and executioner. The best I could do was plead insanity and hope for a reduced sentence and getting time off for good behavior. *God, where are you? I know the word says no weapon formed against me shall prosper.* I remember trying to get that scripture out, not out loud, but in my head.

It was there, but it was stuck. I also remember the feeling of the welts forming on my flesh. Weapons form welts.

God, I asked where you were, but you had to have been nearby because through the ordeal, as I tried to protect my face, you protected my life. I knew no matter what my body endured that my face had to be protected. I didn't wear much makeup and my face was a part of my advertising campaign. I can still hear the hateful things he said to me ringing in my ears all these years later. My God, I survived it though. I survived it all. I didn't cry because that would show weakness.

But as I retell the experience to myself, the tears come, and I feel the saltiness looking through blurred vision at my face in the mirror. She must feel the pain also after all these years because she is crying with me. Help us father. He beat me until his voice ran out of insults and then he just kept hitting. Somehow I got to the door and ran out in the rain only to realize my sheet had fallen off.

I was in the rain naked trying to get back in, begging him to let me in, not knowing what I'd face. All I heard was the door lock. I tried covering my nakedness and was helpless. I thought that he'd let me in the door in a minute, but that minute seemed like an hour. I could see my neighbors peeking through the blinds. They opened their door just enough for me to squeeze through. They gave me a sheet similar to the one I'd been beaten out of, and offered to call the police.

Although I accepted the sheet, I begged them to not call the police. I could tell they were as shocked as I was. While my rescuers tried to comfort me, I heard the door slam and then our car started up. I looked out the window, watching him speed away. I ran out one door into another. I quickly dressed, grabbed a few items and hit it. I knocked on the kind neighbors door, but apparently they were out of kindness and didn't want to get involved further.

I ran to a payphone, called my father and asked him to pick me up. I hid in the bushes until I could see the car and hear the soft beep-beep all clear signal. I was wet and bruised but free. I was scared but free. I was feenin' for a hit, the upper, the downer, anything to feel something different than what I was currently feeling.

It turns out that my father was house-sitting for someone he knew who lived in downtown Charleston. He was a caretaker of sorts. He and a couple of family/friends took me there. I was kept there for a week, sick as two dogs but I was safe. Vomiting up my insides but I was safe.

I remember pleading with those who watched me 24 hours a day to let me go live my life; at the same time I was pleading with you, God, to take my life. I was delusional. I went through horrible withdrawal. I wanted to die, and I fought to live. I cried a lot. I smelled a lot. I prayed a lot. My father reached out to my mom. She said I could come home. But if I couldn't face her before I left, I damn sure couldn't face her knowing that now my actions were far worse than they ever had been. I just couldn't.

My mother's sister lived in Milwaukee and as a favor to my mother, she said I could stay with her and her family. So, after a week, my dad got me a ticket and packed some sandwiches and sodas. He knew not to give me money to travel with because I'd have gotten off at the first stop to find dope.

Actually, I remember thinking I don't need money. Why would I need cash when I have coochie? But I didn't get off that bus. It took about two days to get from Charleston to Milwaukee, although it seemed longer. It probably would have been a shorter trip if not for all the stops. I don't think I've been able to ride a Greyhound without reliving that nightmare to freedom. My father will always be my hero for that. My mother gave me life, but my father did too.

The condensation on the mirror started to break up and separate on its own. There was no need for me to do anything but stand and be brave, all the while being comfortable with who I am, inside and out. My eyes focused on the image in the mirror and stopped at the place where my heart lived. I'd always thought I had a big heart. So big that I should be able to see it beating, rising to a place just under my skin, but I couldn't. The reality was that sometimes I struggled just to feel it even with my hand placed over it during a quiet moment.

As large as my heart is, it doesn't work well. I felt a gradual change years ago, but didn't take the time to get properly diagnosed. Why? I suppose there were several reasons. Maybe it was because of my thinking about a lot of things that hurt me over the years. If I push through the pain, I can get to pain-free. It was like hearing a noise in the car and turning up the radio, so the noise doesn't exist. I'd put my cape on every day and go about the business of being a she-ro, saving everyone but myself. Speaking life into everyone but myself. Cheering for others to live while I was dying.

One night five years ago, when I couldn't take the pain in my body anymore, and could barely breathe or stand, I called a friend to take me to the emergency room. I couldn't drive myself. When I arrived at the hospital, the doctor said two things that changed my life. He asked, "how have you been functioning like this" and then he said, "if you had stayed home one more hour you'd have died of a massive heart attack or stroke." My blood pressure was sky high, my body was drowning in its own fluids, and my heart was performing at 25%.

I was admitted immediately, thinking I'd be back home in a couple of days. I was diagnosed with CHF better know was Congestive Heart Failure. That couple of days turned into seven and I was discharged the day before my 50th birthday with a prescription for bed rest and taking sixteen pills per day. At that time, my heart was functioning at 25%. Over the years, with my daily pills, exercise, hope, prayers, herbs, sleep and the hand of you, my God, my heart function got up to about 65%. However it plummeted again, and now those same things don't seem to help.

On the early morning of January 1st, 2018, I was again rushed to the emergency room. As the partygoers were rushing about celebrating the new year that I was struggling to see. I could feel the life force leaving my body as I was only able to take shallow breaths. Each block of traffic seemed like a mile. I prayed to live and again God, you heard and answered me. I was admitted with a 25% heart function and enough fluid in my body to drown me. I was retaining it faster than I could get rid of it.

The doctors were more insistent on surgery to put a pacemaker/defibrillator in my body. They sternly warned that my heart was not strong enough to save itself should it stop beating. I'd used this heart to give so much love. I'd shared it with so many and when I needed it most, there wasn't a lot to take without totally depleting it. Again the tears fell silently as I placed my hand over my heart and pray.

God, please continue to show me grace and mercy. Please continue to be better to me than I've been to myself. I have work to do and I truly believe that most of it involves you and building your kingdom while I remain a vessel to pour out your love.

My hands moved from my heart to my breasts. I cupped them in my hands and thought about the powerful force that they have always been. My titties, as they were referred to in my youth, became grown woman breasts at a young age. They gave nourishment to my babies. They provided comfort and pleasure to countless men and a few women along the way. I learned early that my breasts make a particular statement and I admit, there were many times I let them speak for themselves. When I tried to silence them, I was faced with the fact that they had much to say, even when I willed them to hush and stay in their place.

My hands moved down to my not-so-flat stomach. The core of me contains an atlas of stretch marks. They served as the road maps my children followed to reach their earthly destinations. The c-section scar is symbolic of the door they burst through when they made their high-pitched entrance.

I think back as I rub that scar sometimes. I consider it a battle scar because I fought to get those babies here. Other times, still, when I look at their grown faces (still beautiful babies), I consider it a beauty mark, because it definitely marks the place where beauty entered the world not once, but twice.

As strong as I'd always been and as much I fought in my life, it didn't seem like my body was strong enough to push those God-given beings out vaginally. They had to be removed surgically. I thought for many years that I had failed because of that. Once I saw how awesome they both are, and how close to God they are, I figured that they intentionally wanted to stay where they were because the world was not ready for them.

The reason doesn't matter now, because however they got here, I'm beyond blessed and ever grateful to be their mother. Maybe I loved them so much, I wanted to keep them as close to me as possible, and willed them to stay in even though I knew they couldn't. One of them is already a parent and the other will soon give birth to her first child.

My hands rubbed my tummy and moved to my thighs. I realize that my size had fluctuated a bit. Maybe a big bit over the years. I've been called and answered to fluffy, thick, thoroughbred, healthy, Amazon, brickhouse and likely some names that I've forgotten. Maybe intentionally forgotten, truth be told. My height most likely came from my father's side and my thickness no doubt was a hand-me-down from Mama and her branch of the family tree. As much as I wanted to blame my size on genetics, I have to take some responsibility.

I've not always taken the best care of myself and there were times when I dealt with a real food addiction. Instead of dealing with my emotional issues, I became an emotional eater. It was a yo-yo issue. I'd stop, go back. Stop. Go back. It is not nearly as bad as it used to be, but it still flares up from time to time. When there's stress playing out in a couple of areas of my life; then that stress spills over into other areas, and sometimes that includes what I put into my body.

The fact that I've worked 3rd shift for many years certainly didn't help eliminate stress. Health challenges didn't help. Red flags, rather ignoring all kinds of red flags, didn't help, but God, you and I both know that ultimately most of my stress in life has been brought on by my poor decisions. For that, I only have myself to blame. Free will can be a bitch. I patted my tummy and smiled, because ultimately, even after poor choices, including staying in stressful situations, drug abuse, and prostitution, I managed to conceive a god and a goddess who burst forth from my womb and changed the world for the better, at least my world.

My hips are shapely. My thighs are strong enough to carry me, and what sometimes seems like the weight of the world. My calves are defined with prominent muscles. I earned them by playing basketball and soccer in school and further enhanced them by walking one or two million miles on the stroll back in the day. I can't help but smile when I remember how these legs used to stop traffic and actually caused a fender bender when one distracted man was put under a spell that lasted a second too long.

I remember a pair of red terry-cloth shorts that fit like I was born in them and they just grew with me. I had them on at a truck stop one day. I was bent over the Pac-Man arcade game waiting for my food and I overheard a conversation between two men. The first man asked his friend if he believed in reincarnation after death. The friend said, "no, do you?" The first man said "hell yeah! And when I die I want to come back as a pair of red shorts." Why can I still hear their voices, southern twang and all.

At the time, I turned around and smiled. They paid for my meal and I left feeling quite flattered. Today, the replaying of that scene makes me sick. My legs seemed to be worth so much back then, even with two scars, one from knee surgery and one from an "accident" with a wire hanger. Now, they're sometimes slow and sometimes painful, but still functional, especially for forming a lap for the babies to climb on or rest their heads on at nap time.

As I predicted, I stood in front of the full-length mirror naked, not just in flesh, but in my truths and vulnerabilities. The reflection looked to be more than just an image in glass. It looked at me as if it knew me on more than a surface level. This was not a random reflection. She was me and I was her. We exchanged stares and I realized this was the carrier of the life I left behind more than 30 years ago.

I stood there remembering, critiquing, accepting and owning the life that I saw represented by my reflection, the life that she and I had lived together. I saw the pain, the pitfalls, the perseverance, and suddenly, I was proud. Proud that through it all, I am still standing. I am somewhat still traumatized, but still standing, nonetheless. My wounds, physical and otherwise, are in various states of healing and being erased by time, but I stand proudly in my present time and even in my past.

As I look at my eyes looking back at me, I realize that some of that pride comes from the fact that life has not found a way to eliminate me, to eliminate us. It wasn't able to kill us in our past or in our present. She, my reflection, may have been in limbo while I moved on, but we survived.

I wrapped a towel around my nakedness and reached my hand towards my reflection. I reached for her with love. No shame, no guilt. Just love. I needed to talk to her and I'm sure she needed to talk to me as well. After some time, she took my hand and stepped out of the place she'd been left in decades ago.

I wasn't sure what she'd say, what I'd say, or what we'd say, but I was sure that together, we were more than enough. We sat in the bedroom across from one another to look back at our past and learn, and more importantly to look ahead to our future and live.

As I proceeded to rub myself down with lavender-scented shea butter, my favorite, the me that was in the chair across from my bed looked confused, untrusting, and somewhat scared. I assured her as best as I could that she was safe, finally in a place of no restrictions, abuse, trauma, or self-hatred. I told her that the negativity she had known and carried for decades, was finally lifted from her sagging shoulders. We had carried it for so long that we believed it was a permanent part of us. She clearly was not quick to trust me or take my word.

I couldn't feel some type of way about that; after all, she knew me but at the same time she didn't. As she sat in an uncomfortable silence. I went about my ritual that always occurs after my shower. I was giving her eyes and her mind time to take it all in, to adjust. I was giving her time to accept that yes, we did make it. We lived. We got out. We made it beyond the life that the She of us had known.

This was the first time in thirty-plus years that she had realized that. She knew that she lived outside of the death that she had been trapped in, only able to see herself. I tried not to look her directly in the eyes because I didn't want to scare her or embarrass her. I didn't want her to know that through my own silent tears, I noticed hers.

After some time of business, partly out of necessity and partly to kill time and create space, I sat opposite her and eventually the me that was her broke the silence.

Part Three

Reflections

"**H**ey," she said, "I have some questions." I knew her questions would be many. "Where have we been? Where did we go when we first left? What took you so long to come get me? Did we ever come to know real love? Do the bruises ever heal? Do the nightmares stop? Did we ever get married? Did we stay clean and really leave the drugs alone? Did we have children?"

Her questions were nonstop. Perhaps the most significant ones focused on how did we become who we were in the past? Who are we now and what took you so long to come back and get me?

"Why didn't you come get me sooner and pull me from the perpetual memories that represented the hell we lived in?"

Hearing her questions caused my mind and hers to spiral in a million different directions. What started as slow tears for both of us simultaneously erupted into a river, what I would call a bursting of the floodgates. Rivers of living water accompanied by sobs of relief as if we were finally able, together, to take a complete exhale.

Every pain was released from past and present. It was as if every ache was being announced. Every scab, full or partial, was being ripped away and every fresh wound and assault from life was magnified. I'd had time to at least partially process but the She of me had not, and I had to meet my sister self where she was.

We cried together until the sound was inaudible. The tears dried up and through swollen red eyes, we communicated in silence for a while, each lost in her own thoughts. Each thought was a piece of the puzzle that was us. Finally, present me spoke.

"I'm sorry that I left you in that dark place for so long. I'm sorry I was never strong enough to travel back and get you, to tell you that we made it and survived. I'm sorry that I let you relive that nightmare over and over. I'm sorry I didn't come back so that we could work together to forgive, if not forget. I'm sorry I left you there when maybe we could have learned together from our past and lived our future."

"But please understand, Sis, it's never too late. I want to tell you and the rest of the world that whenever the opportunity presents itself we have to try. Even near death we can feel the presence of life somehow, in the smallest way and that has to be enough to grab onto. It is enough to grab onto."

"Sis I need you to know that I thought of you every day. I never felt complete without you. I thought of you every time I did adult shit. I wanted you to be proud of me. I thought of you when I fell in love, got a real 9-to-5, and started getting paid weekly or biweekly instead of by the hour or sexual request."

"I thought of you every time I made the smallest accomplishment. I thought of you when I voted, paid bills, got a car and got oil changes, went to get a physical, and got my necessary HIV test every six months for the first ten years after leaving the street. I'm sorry I didn't come back to tell you that the nightmares didn't stop, but they don't happen as often. I'm sorry that the you of us felt that the me of us abandoned you."

"I'm sorry you haven't met our children. Yes, we have children, one girl, one boy. They are awesome and even though I never felt I deserved any part of them, they came through me. They love me, us, with our flaws, imperfections and the many mistakes I've made raising them. They have approved of and supported me through it all. There have been times that they suffered with me like the troopers they are, and times where as much as I hate to admit it, they've suffered because of me or decisions I made."

"If they've ever been disappointed in me, they never let me see it in their eyes. In fact, all I've ever seen in their eyes is love for me and genuine concern for my well-being. They've done their best to love me, not because of, but in spite of. They made me feel like I could walk on water when in reality, I could barely crawl on land."

"I'm sorry I left you suspended in limbo and wondering what happened to us while I found a way to run ahead and see what the end is going to be. I know you were afraid to even think too much about a future because all you had was a present that perpetually consisted of the past. I know for us that there were happy times, good days and laughter long ago. Wouldn't you agree that for a brief time we had a normal childhood? But then again, what is the definition of normal?"

"What we called our normal life turned dark and ugly, covered by a curtain so heavy that we were almost suffocated. It seemed to get heavier by the day until it finally smothered us both, and we lived under that weight of darkness, even though we tried to fight it off."

"Somehow we learned to live, or rather exist, in that stale, light-deprived, toxic place. Please know that once I escaped, I prayed for you. I stood in the gap for you. I got on my bended knees to pray for you because I knew that every time you thought about being on bended knees, there was nothing spiritual going on."

"I worked hard to redeem your character. I faked it until I made it. I was good at that, after all. We had lots of experiences faking it, didn't we? I worked three jobs at one time to raise those children of ours, not making with those three checks every two weeks what we used to clear in two good days. Hell, sometimes one."

"I was part-time here, part-time there. Here. There. Everywhere. It sounds funny but it isn't. When I tell you I struggled, I mean I struggled. I tried to keep an okay appearance on the outside but inside, I was not okay. We were not okay. I felt like if you ever found out what happened to us that I wanted you to be proud. Proud of me, proud of us. Finally proud of us."

"I wanted someone who knew me before I became The Queen to be proud of me. I joined churches for and studied different religions for you. I did that because I knew that the you of us had given up on believing in God long ago. To be honest, we both probably thought, at one time, that he had given up on us. They say what doesn't kill you will make you stronger. If that is the case, we ought to be ready for the weight-lifting category in the world Olympics."

"I want you to know we even married for a while. It was for the wrong reasons which was why I'd done many other things. I thought it was something that would make me seem more normal. You know they (whoever *they* are) say you can't turn a hoe into a housewife. I wanted to prove them wrong. It didn't last, but for a while we lived the married life. We had a wedding ring, a ceremony, a new last name, and another fresh start which, after some time, got very stale."

"While you were stuck in time, Sis, I've spent years, so much time, looking for a fresh start. I finally realized that wherever I go, I take us with me. After all these years, I still get the desire for a fresh start sometimes. What I haven't yet figured out is exactly what I'm looking for. I guess I'm hoping that once I fill you in, we can figure that out together."

"I only know that on the quest, I've gotten better. Maybe that is it. Isn't that what we should be looking for? To get better? I met a dear old woman who always claimed that whenever someone asked how she was doing, she'd respond 'I'm getting better all the time.' The world could be crashing in and she'd still respond the same way. She believed that our perception is our reality."

"Either way, I'm glad we are now here together to figure it out. The look you're giving me tells me you don't quite trust me. I understand that, but I hope in time you will. After all, I'm you and you are me. Without each other, neither of us would exist. Please give me a chance. I'd ask you to give me time, but I can't. You've already waited more than thirty years. I tried to see you. I knew you were there but every time I looked in the mirror, I'd get physically sick. It wasn't you; it was me. I guess that line is true sometimes."

"Beloved, I knew you were there, somewhere stranded on the road at the intersection of then and now. I couldn't see clearly enough to get a grip and get you out. I prayed for strength to go back, go deeper, see clearer, and be able to release you. I am ashamed that I have to admit that every time God sent me strength, I turned it into guilt, shame, self-judgment, fear of rejection, and self-doubt. The weight of all of that kept me paralyzed in the present, unable to reach back in the past; yet, I constantly lived in the past. Yes, I know that is messed up for real."

"I asked myself countless times, what if I went back for you and got stuck there myself? I will forever ask your forgiveness because I sacrificed the you of us so the me of us could live. It was never my intention but that is ultimately what happened. I know my apology is weak, but it is all I have to offer you. That and my truth."

"Why now? That's a good question. I will try to give you an honest answer to that one before I begin to answer the countless other questions you have about our life. I'm going to be as honest as I can and please keep in mind that this is new and scary for me too, almost as much as it is for you."

"I came to a place a few years ago where I finally started to see my true worth, not in my potential but in my present as I was. Up until then, I pretended to know but I really didn't, because I could not see my contribution to making the world a better place. Periodically I'd get trapped where you were, it was just too dark, and I didn't stay long enough to find you.

"I think our relationship with our mother was never what we wanted it to be. I am not blaming her; may she rest in peace. I'm just stating the facts. I'd remember that the best relationships we had with men lasted just a few minutes, literally and figuratively. Those relationships were based on transactions or trade. Those relationships taught us that all money isn't green, nobody does anything without a payoff, and fair exchange is no robbery. I said all that to say that relationships were never our strong area, including the one with self."

"I know I'm rambling but I'm trying to get it all out, so my mind and my mouth are trying to catch up with each other. Somehow, everything I'm telling you will answer all of your questions. I remember how ashamed I was when I had to get a GED because I stupidly dropped out of high school a few weeks before graduation. I think about the fact that if my babies needed a blood transfusion, some official-looking professional would tell me I was not a candidate because of my drug use and the resulting hepatitis."

"I remember all the times I tried to brush my teeth, wash my face, or do something with my hair in as little light as possible. Sometimes I'd do it in the dark and play it off when some kind soul told me later that I had toothpaste on my chin. I think about all those things and more and realize how far I've come in every area of our life. I am surely not where I want to be, but I damn sure am not where I used to be. So, the time is now, now or never."

"You see as bad as it had been, it isn't what it used to be now. Does that make sense? When I found a way to dissect all that I had carried, I was able to see how I survived it. The drug habit has been gone for almost thirty-five years now. The hepatitis is cured because we were selected as one of a few from thousands to try a new medication that would have been too expensive for me. I got my GED, passed up a 4-year-degree and later in life, through my employer, I applied for and was granted a scholarship. I actually had the highest scoring application in the company that year."

"I went to college a year or so off that scholarship, got good grades in my classes, and dropped out. Why? Because it was like another job and I really had no aspirations in relationship to a career. I just wanted to do it to prove that I could."

"Our son survived a life-threatening disease. In fact, he was a Make-A-Wish child. He is still here years later and didn't need a drop of blood from me. We've been evicted and now we own a 3-bedroom home. We don't have a mortgage on that home, we own it."

"The nightmares we used to have every night and then every week don't happen as often anymore. Did I think my life was perfect? Absolutely not. But I was winning. *We* were winning. It dawned on me that at one time we were victims but now we could call ourselves victors. We, you and I, have earned that right and I need you to know that."

"So, here we are together to uncover and discover. I got strong enough and I owed it to you, to me, to our babies, to those who are in the midst of this process, and to our God who created us and saved us, to come get you. I owed it to our mother, who lost a child, to make sure we weren't lost. Not if we could help it. I owed it to our father who once said, *'if you serve God's people, he will enhance your life.'* We have been doing that and God has enhanced our life. At one time, we made decisions that were slowly killing us, *but God.*"

"Sis, we are examples of the last shall be first. We shall live and not die, at least not with a needle stuck in our arm, at least not thrown out on a street corner having been killed by a trick, at least not from a life-sucking disease that ate us up when we opened up. I could not leave you there knowing I had not done right by you. We've both paid the price, with interest."

"I came to a place where I had to admit, I've likely lived more years than I have left to live. Although anything is possible, considering our dad is alive and kicking in his early 90s, still raking the yard every day and washing the Cadillac every other day by hand. One of his brothers lived to be ninety-six. Whatever years we have left, you and I, we are going to live with joy, looking ahead to every opportunity and every hurdle to overcome. I don't know God's plans, so I want to get some things in order and mending my relationship with you is at the top of the list."

"My apologies may come off lackluster, but they are the same apologies I gave to myself. I don't want either of us to live anymore looking for forgiveness, but instead for favor. What? What did you say? Oh, you want to know how it all started. You want to go back to the beginning. Sure. Maybe that will help us both create an opening where we will find some deeper closure."

"Do you mind if I sit a little closer to you? I know you may not fully trust this whole experience, but if we can be closer it will help us to get closer. Thanks. The fact that you're reaching out your hand to me means so much. I promise not to come any closer than you are comfortable with. We both know what it feels like for people to invade our space – physically, mentally, and spiritually. Please chime in when you have a question or something to add. Your voice matters, too."

"I have several theories as to when and why things went wrong. It's funny because at different points in my life, in our life, those theories have changed. Maybe together we can come to a point where we both see the same thing. They say a lot, but two heads can be better than one."

"I don't know about you, but my earliest memories are of us and our family living in Japan. Daddy was stationed there. So we went too, us and Mama. It just so happens our baby brother was born there. I always thought that was so funny. I used to tease him, telling him that, like an imported vase or something, it said *Made in Japan* on his butt. It's nice to see you laugh about that."

"I can remember it being crowded there. It might be stereotypical, but in my mind, they all looked the same in Japan. You're shaking your head. That must mean we were in the same page, even then. You still don't believe this is real? Me either, but it is, more than 30 years later it is. We also lived in Hawaii for a while. Do you remember that? No? Well, we did."

"Actually, we went back when our son was a Make-a-Wish child. The doctors weren't sure he'd survive the rare blood disorder he had. His wish was to go to Hawaii and swim with the dolphins. So the four of us, our son, daughter, their father, and you and I were flown to Hawaii for a week. I have a picture of them with the dolphins hanging up and every time I've moved it's one of the first things I hang up."

"Yes, I see. We're getting off course and rambling. That will probably happen a lot because we have so much to cover. Did I mention to you that we lost him to liver cancer a few years ago? Our brother, that is. He was a heavy drinker. He stopped drinking but the hepatitis had already started. It attacked his liver and turned to cancer. He got active in church before he died. There is tissue on the plant stand next to you. Please hand me one also."

"Sometimes I think that I've cried my last tear over him and then, like now, I talk about him or just remember, and the tears come back. I know that as I fill you in on our life that we'll talk about this again. It was such a pivotal point in our life; it seems to appear in a sentence on each page since it happened. Speaking over his casket was the hardest thing I'd ever done, until I spoke over Mama's casket."

"Her casket was one she chose and was very simple. There were flowers everywhere. I remember looking at them thinking about how our grandma always said *give me my flowers while I yet live.* I think back to those two days, our brother's funeral and our mother's funeral and first thought is that I didn't know it was possible to have the air sucked out of your lungs, not once but twice, and still live. But, as I stood representing us, I realized that it is possible."

"I know you remember our childhood. At least the part of it that could be classified as a childhood, before we started growing up too quickly, largely due to our own decisions, and the consequences of those decisions. They who seem to say a lot, say that youth is the best time of our life. This time I have to agree with what they say. We just don't realize it until those years are gone and we've moved on, giving up something we can't get back."

"Now that we are in our mid-50s, I often look back and wonder how things would have been different if things would have been different. I suppose you don't really have an opinion on that, since, for you, our life stopped progressing and has been stuck at the place where I left you. I've experienced more than fifty years of life while the you of us has not experienced more than 22 years of life. I find myself constantly wanting to apologize for leaving you. I know. I know you're trying to understand, and I appreciate you telling me that. It helps. It really does."

"I can't stop looking at you. You're beautiful. I guess I didn't see how beautiful because on the occasion that I did look in the mirror, I looked past you or through you, as if you weren't there. I was in denial on many days and I convinced myself that the years you represented did not exist."

"Honestly, for me, that was a coping mechanism I used for years. I'd go in and out, between denial and acceptance, until little by little, I began to spend more time in the reality that yes, you did exist. We existed and our life together did indeed happen, just as I remembered it."

"It took years, decades, but now I can fully accept and fully heal while helping you to heal as well. What? What did you say? Did I feel incomplete? Of course I did. Most of my life, I didn't feel like I really fit in. Once I got grown, left our life and started a new one, I still didn't feel like I fit in. I had a good life. I became quite popular. We've always been a people magnet. That was one of the things that sustained us during childhood, and it made us very good at our chosen hustle. Well, once I left you and went legit, that continued. I think that is a gift from God and should be used for good."

"To be honest Sis, I've never seen what others see when they look at me, at us. But, I know it's there. I see it in action. I see the way others react to it in us. So, to answer your question, yes, I felt incomplete. I think, no, I'm sure, that I felt that even when we were together. I wish I could talk without jumping all over the place or give you short, simple answers to your questions. But I can't. For so long, these answers and stories have been bottled up together. It's almost as if they have become one concoction – a little of this, a pinch of that."

"You know people judge things based on their perception. They look at us, at me, and see what they see, and they think it looks good and want some portion of that. But they look through a limited lens. They want what they believe is the prize but don't want the process. They want the perceived power but not the personal pain. I think we wore happy like a mask for part of our childhood."

"I've been able to fake it until I could make it using half my strength to smile and the other half to push down the tears that always threatened to burst through the dam of life and crumble the wall that I've spent so much time building up to protect us from the outside world. Anyway, back to our childhood. Our parents were married and to my knowledge, neither one had children besides us and our brother. I don't have solid proof, but in my spirit I always felt like Mama lost a baby at some point, through a miscarriage before or after us. I don't know why I feel that. I never had the nerve to talk to her about it. We didn't have that kind of relationship. Maybe I saw or heard something that gave me that idea. If so, like so many other things, perhaps I blocked it out."

"Do you remember when they divorced? I do, vaguely. We were six. I remember a house with an upstairs. I can tell by the look on your face that you remember it too. I can still hear bits and pieces of harsh words, mostly from Mama. Daddy never has been one to get too loud for too long. He always spoke volumes with his silence and actions. I don't remember him putting up much of a fight to stay."

"When it was unpleasant, I didn't think about it much, but as I got older, I wondered why he didn't fight to stay. Why didn't he fight for his kids, his family? But then again, maybe he did. You see, I've learned over the years that what passes for one thing, sometimes, is really something else, and that the greatest fight can come from surrendering. That was one of the tougher lessons I had to learn. So tough, in fact, that I had to learn it more than once."

"Mama tried to teach us to sew, but we weren't interested. One of our community daughters is an amazing seamstress, very gifted. Every time I support her business or see her work, I think of our mother and that sewing machine that turned fabric into finery. She was good. Better than good."

"My daughter, excuse me, our daughter, still has a bathrobe Mama made her when she was a little girl. She actually had a tiny piece of it sewn into her wedding dress to honor Mama and feel her presence. Her sewing was one of the things I admired about our mother. I like watching her sew. I also liked to watch her play the piano. Especially when she'd pull out the old hymn books and play while us and grandma would sing."

"Our grandmother would sing loud and in the right key. I think that is when I personally liked her voice the most. We, of course, would get in where we fit in. I suppose it's not bragging to you, but we were gifted with a beautiful voice. When we three generations got together and let everyone with a voice praise the Lord, it was even more beautiful."

"Back to Mama and Daddy. We missed him in the house but would spend weekends with him, and watch Soul Train every Saturday morning. We created our own dance line down the middle of the living room. Our brother always made fun of the dancers and then he tried to imitate them. I smile remembering how clumsy he was. He never did learn how to dance, but like us, he could sing."

"I don't remember the exact year that daddy moved back down south. Do you? No. Well, I know that we were still young when he went back to his home state, South Carolina. Once he moved we visited every year in the summer. We had so much fun. Daddy knew some people that we thought were really cool. They bypassed friends and became family almost immediately. They helped take care of us and were extremely protective of us. They spoiled us at every opportunity. They made Soul Train even more fun for us because our dance line got longer. I can tell you remember that, don't you?"

"You may or may not be surprised to know that our father still keeps a house full of people. His home is almost like a boarding house. Our brother hated that. But, I think you and I have always understood that this is his way. He has always felt there is one more corner for one more person. I guess we get it because we have lived like that as well, especially once the children came along. Our house was a gathering house after school, and on the weekends."

"Once our kids got older, we almost ran a rooming house, of sorts. There always seemed to be an extra child or two. Some stayed a night, some stayed a few nights, and one in particular staying until we moved. And then he moved with us. We made a room in the attic and then we moved again and made a room for him in the basement."

"Of course, he is grown now, but still family and will fight anyone who says he's not. The day we found out our son was going to be a father; we went and got the child's mother and brought her home to our place. We moved our son to the couch and put her in his room and took care of her until after the baby was born. So, yeah, we get daddy's way of thinking. Oh yes, we always notified parents in the case where there was parents, grandparents, or whoever was responsible for the young person. "

"Even now, when there are family dinners at my house, every chair, couch, and seat is taken. Some even take turns standing, playing musical chairs because family is so much more than who we marry or are connected to through birth. It is who we love and live for. I can't wait for you to get to know the family, the bonus children and grandchildren. I know you'll love them as much as I do. They will love you too, because to them I, you and I, can't do much wrong, and when we do, they're not often willing to bring that up."

"Oh, it is nice to see you genuinely smile. Anyway, when we went to visit our father in Charleston, he would take us to spend time on the family farm in Laurens. It was quite different from the city. There was a red dirt road from the main road to the house. We helped feed the chickens. We'd ride the plow mule, pick fruit from the peach tree, pull peanuts from the ground to wash them and boil them in saltwater, and pull watermelons out of the ground and let them get good and cold."

"Remember we had to wear gloves to cut okra and when we didn't our hands would itch until they hurt? Once in a while, the farmhouse would get invaded by a directionally challenged snake or a frog would hop in while we children ran in and out of the door. We'd help slop the hogs one day only to watch them be slaughtered the next and turned into bacon, ham and pork chops. We were taught to give thanks for every creature that gave its life to sustain ours."

"I think I speak for us and our brother Jay when I say that the best times were in the evenings when the adults would sit on the porch trying to catch anything that resembled a breeze while the children would try to catch lightening bugs. We each had our own mason jar with the lid. We'd catch them, stare and wonder at who had the brighter bug and then let them go only to repeat the process. Some of them were almost as big as light bulbs, not the regular light bulbs but the smalls one that lit our night light."

"The adults teased us about the night lights sometimes, but we didn't care. It was better than us risking snakes wrapping around our legs or slithering up out of the toilet with our butts as the bullseye they aimed for. We laugh now, but it wasn't so funny back then. It makes me happy to see you laugh and smile. I know when I left you, it was with more tears than laughter. I'm sorry for that and I know I've said it a million times, so many times that it almost seems diluted. But, Sister-Self, if you only knew how sorry I am, you'd know how much weight my apology carries."

"I find it interesting that what made you smile like that was us talking about the days on the farm down south. Those days spent hanging out with our cousins were the best. You know Daddy had a large family. What? Yes, he is still alive. I thought I mentioned that, maybe not. But, even if I did, it's okay because I know as fast as I'm giving out information, you are trying to process it. It doesn't matter because we are going to keep at it until I've said all I feel like I need to say, and you've heard all you need to hear."

"We did talk about it, when I talked about the fact that he keeps people around all the time. The fact that he is over 90 means it is worth saying and being grateful for over and over. Our father, thank God, is still alive and he loves us both, you and I. He never separated us, but loved us for who we were at any given moment. Girl, he still drives, washes the car by hand, and rakes the yard every day. I don't like him driving because his sight is dimming, and he doesn't always like to wear his hearing aid. Believe it or not, he still has two sisters living and both are older than him. It's crazy. We've got some long lives in our family tree. Who knows? We might be able to live to a ripe old age."

"No. No, she is not. Remember I talked about her funeral earlier. Yeah, she has been gone about three years now. She died in the hospital. Her heart gave out and she didn't want heroic measures used to save her. She was ready to go. I talked to her the day before. Funny, she died on a Sunday morning. I was up, looking at a video on my phone of her going through her house for the first time after I had a crew clean and remodel it. It looked like a new house with new everything. She was so happy."

"When the doctor called me from a Minnesota hospital to tell me she had died, I asked what time. The time he gave was the exact time I had been randomly watching the video of her in her happy place. The happiest I believe that I've ever seen her. I know. I knew it was no coincidence. It was divine intervention. There is no such thing in my mind as a coincidence, only God remaining anonymous. He knew what was about to happen and wanted me to be in as good a place as possible when it did."

"Mama's only brother died not long before she did. Now the only sibling left is her younger sister. I moved here temporarily to stay with her for six months or so while I grew strong in my sobriety, with the expectation that I'd move back to Charleston. I never did. When? I arrived in Milwaukee August 8th of 1985."

"Ironically, that was Mama's birthday. I think again that was the hand of God and it happened that way so that I would always remember the start of that chapter of our life. When it came to her death, God not only put me in front of a video with her happiness filling the screen, but Mama died on our daddy's birthday. December 18th. I can never be saddened by her death without turning that in to being happy for our father's life."

"As a child, we often heard Grandma say that He never gives us more than we can bear. I have a plaque hanging in the house that says, 'God may not give you what you can handle, but He will help you handle what you are given.' I believed when I came here that I'd be able to come back for you in six months. Where in the world did I get that from? I thought I'd have killed my demons. I thought the wounds would be healed."

"I guess that just shows how deep trauma can go, how far beneath the surface of us those wounds can cut. I've heard it said that time heals all wounds. Bullshit. Time heals wounds if you do the work. Time heals all wounds if you are honest and can look in the mirror and have reflections with your reflection. It heals all wounds if you develop a relationship with your higher power. Time heals all wounds if you remove yourself from the path of the weapon that injured you. Time alone won't do it."

"You see, I had to dig to uncover secrets and pains I'd buried and confront the life I wanted to act like didn't exist. I had to make excuses as to why I couldn't give blood during the blood drives at the hospital I worked at for almost 16 years. I stayed up late only to get up early, telling myself that the less I slept, the less the nightmares would come. I had to learn to be okay with a regular sex life and accept that sometimes I would cry afterwards, because although I wanted emotional intimacy, I cringed inside at being touched on the outside."

"I wondered daily if I'd done enough to redeem my life, if God had forgiven me and how I could begin to forgive myself. That takes time and for me, the work continues. But I'm strong enough now to pull you from your bondage so I can share my healing with you and together we can go forward. I won't always go into detail when people ask me how I got where I am. They ask that only because of what they perceive about my life. When people come for prayer or counsel, I don't often go into details but in both cases, my message is the same. Transformation is possible at any stage of the game."

"Hmm, The Queen hasn't always been The Queen, or maybe we were a queen and just didn't know it. Miracles happen every day; healing happens every day. When we follow the process, which can be slow, progress is happening even when we don't see it. The caterpillar does not become a butterfly overnight, but still they are two creatures in one, two lifetimes in one life. That ritual of nature applies to us as well."

"No, I'm not a preacher by any means, maybe a teacher who has learned some hard lessons along the way. But then again, I think most of us fall in that category. Do you remember when we went to a private catholic school for our elementary and middle school years? After one year of public education, Mama thought it was best for us to get the type of education she thought we should have. During those years, we had very few classmates. It wasn't even enough to qualify for as a handful, and there weren't any teachers of color. But we, and our brother, survived those years because we went home to an afterschool life with what I often thought of as our functional dysfunctional Black family."

"Do you remember how at a young age we always had a feeling that we didn't seem to fit in to any of our worlds? At school or at home? I look back and I've learned to acknowledge feelings and not dismiss them without inspection. It was a very real feeling that became a normal feeling and we certainly didn't know what to do with it. So we learned to live with that nagging voice always in the back of our mind. Once we got to public high school, our differences were even more apparent. We'd worn uniforms to school for years and didn't know how to dress. We spoke differently because Mama insisted we speak proper English. Slang was not allowed. The debate and speech team were a part of our curriculum."

"The proper English confuses people sometimes. I've worked primarily in some type of customer service role, and based on my conversation, many people have assumed I was a white woman. It is so obvious once they meet me. You can tell by their mannerisms and their response that they are surprised to be standing next to a Black woman. Sometimes, I'd answer the phone with a standard greeting and people wouldn't leave a message, they'd hang up. If they called right back, I would ask why they hung up and they'd answer with *I thought you were an answering machine and at first I didn't want to leave a message.* I don't know what is worse, to be thought of as a different person or not a person at all."

"It's probably one of my biggest secrets, Sis, but since leaving you I still wonder if I fit in. To solve that concern, I think I developed what might be my gift. I get people to fit in with me. From the outside looking in, it probably looks like I draw people to me and we certainly do. We seem to be the type that people just gravitate to. I genuinely do want everyone I come in contact with to think they're special, and they do. One of my longtime friends says that she has never seen someone with friends from so many different walks of life."

"However, underneath all that, behind it at all, there is still that voice that will annoyingly occasionally whisper words of discontent to me. *Are you good enough? What do you have to offer them?* Since leaving you, I've spent a great deal of time wondering what my purpose is. Most days. I believe that I've come to the conclusion that our purpose is very simple – to love and in doing so, make this world a better place."

"It sounds like a fortune cookie or an overused cliché, but I believe it to be true. I will admit though that unconditional love is hard sometimes, at least for me. When I feel like that, I have to remember the times someone loved me, loved us, not because of, but in spite of."

"A lot of people won't understand that, but I get it now. Our mother loved us, but I don't think she always liked us. Or at least she didn't like what we did with our life. I'm not sure she ever forgave us for leaving her house at fifteen, dropping out of high school, and giving up a free college education to become a drug-addicted prostitute who rented her body and sold services that I'd never perform or participate in with a clear, sober mind. As our son would say, *help us father.*"

"I've learned, Sis, that sometimes that is all I can say. Help us father. Mama wouldn't have called us prostitute, whore, or hooker. She'd say 'lady of the night' or that we were fast, but not free. That sounded more delicate to her. She also used to say that young ladies don't fart, they fluff, and they don't sweat they glisten. She had quite a way with words. Maybe that is where we get it from. Oh, that's right, you don't know. I mean, you know that we've always loved to read and write. Remember when Mama would come in our room at night and fuss because we'd have a flashlight under the covers trying to read when we were supposed to be sleep?"

"Yeah, it is funny now, but it wasn't so funny back then. We wrote poetry but very seldom share it. We wrote about love, life, and relationships. I think it is funny that we wrote about male/female relationships because we aren't experts on the subject. We even wrote erotic poetry. Now that, I consider us to be experts at. Oh, you think that's funny, too. Girl, listen, we know what we know, and we like what we like."

"Over the years, we have written very personal pieces for specific people. We wrote pieces for marriage, illness, death, divorce, births, hard times, and birthdays. I run into people years after they've received a piece and they'll tell me its' still framed and hanging on their wall or on a shelf where they can see it every day. No, it's not something I am paid to do. I do it as the spirit leads me to do so. When people request one, I have to pray about it and ask for words from the divine source. It never takes too long. If it does then I can't do it. It shouldn't be hard, but easy and authentic."

"I thought that once you were freed, we could work together to start a greeting card company or open a small coffee shop with a small reading corner that sells homemade treats like muffins and banana bread. I think we'd be good at greeting cards, but we're not illustrators. I had a live-in relationship with an amazing free-hand artist. He was locked up for some months and would write to me. He'd also draw pictures on my envelopes. I saved all his letters. Once the relationship was over, as I was going through the heartache, I finally threw the letters away, but I kept the envelopes."

"Why? I felt the envelopes were a better representation of the best of him. Our breakup took me years to get over. Baby, when I tell you I mourned that relationship, please believe me. I finally had to let go of the envelopes. Holding onto them was holding on to a piece of him that was no longer mine, and I needed to focus on my present, not my past. It was best at the time, but I wish I'd held on to at least one. He has left this earth and taken his gift with him."

"I actually helped him get a contract doing card cover illustrations for a community member. He was paid a good price, but my artist, who lacked a regular income, decided he wanted to draw only what he wanted to draw, and he quit. I was not only embarrassed, but I was furious as well. I had to admit that I was largely responsible, because I tolerated that behavior."

"I've learned many lessons, even in the difficult times. One that sticks is that we teach people how to treat us based on what we tolerate and how we treat our self. I loved him, but the way I loved him changed. Even with all we went through and how long it took me to get over him, when they closed that casket, a piece of me was in there and I felt it being ripped out. I'm glad you missed having to endure that."

"There is so much I want to tell you; my thoughts are swimming in my head all on top of one another. I knew it was time we talked, you and I, but I prepared no outline or bullet points for this conversation. Our early school years were uneventful for the most part. We were intelligent and got good grades, but we did our share of cuttin' up too. We weren't necessarily bad, but we were the ringleader of a small group of the older kids who occasionally hung out by the creek to drink wine on the weekend. Our parents or someone's parents would drop us off at the mall for a movie."

"Yep, that's right. We didn't always go to the movie. I know. I think back about that now and I laugh. We lived equally in the two worlds. The white world and the black world, our world. Actually, we became very ingrained in the white world, so that was our world, too. We had white playmates and classmates, white teachers, even largely white radio stations. At home, we did have exposure to Black artists and their music. But we also grew up listening to and liking Hall & Oates, Fleetwood Mac, Bee Gees, even Elton John. We alternated between that and our music. Daddy's favorite two artists had to be Bobby Womack and Al Green."

"There weren't a ton of Blacks in Duluth, where we lived, but we had our Calvary Baptist Church family and we had our trips down south. We also had the influence of Mama's parents, who helped raise us. We lived with them at one time. Granddaddy was such a wise man. He was so big and strong in some ways and in others, very gentle. Our grandmother on the other hand, not so much. All the grandchildren and some adults had a fear of her wrath. She was stern and not nearly as outwardly loving as Granddaddy."

"We always tried being extra quiet around her. She used to put the small TV on top of the big TV so she could watch two of her daytime soaps at one time. That was long before 'picture in picture' or before we could DVR everything to watch later. Yes, girl, that is a thing now. I would bet with assurance that our grandkids have two times more things recorded at our house than I do."

"Speaking of our grandkids, I don't know if I was clear about that earlier. Our son has an eight-year-old and our daughter is currently pregnant. But we claim two grandkids because our children have three sisters on their father's side. I was instrumental in raising one of those girls. Her mother took off when she turned one and at that time, the baby went home with me. I helped their father raise her and treated her like one of my own. Loved her like one of my own. Combed her hair like one of my own. Raised her like one of my own."

"Anyway, she grew up and took on a lifestyle I wasn't proud of and got pregnant. Yes, we were there in the hospital when she had her baby, a beautiful little girl who will argue you down if you tell her I'm not Grandma Clara. Her mother's decision to lead an irresponsible life that's not conducive to motherhood has left Eva in our care for long periods of time. Between her grandfather, myself, and our two children, she has all she needs and some of what she wants."

"The other side of her family doesn't have much to do with her. Eva's maternal grandmother is in and out when it is convenient to her. But as far as the day-to-day, she can't be counted on. What? Do I resent that? Absolutely. I resent the entire situation. I resent Eva's mother for not making better choices. I resent her mother's side of the family for not being active in her life like she's not out here in the world. I resent Eva's father even though I'm not one hundred percent sure who that is. We think we know, but it wouldn't be obvious if we calculated it based on his presence in her life."

"Eva's grandfather and I have become a part of a growing group of grandparents who are taking on the responsibility to raise our grandkids. We don't get to be grandparents but instead become parents again. No, our other grand is cared for by his parents. In that case, I get to be a grandmother, sometimes an overbearing one but I'm okay with that."

"Oh, our grandmother! Yes, she was something else. She used to bake pound cake from scratch every week. We would get to take turns licking the spoon and scraping the bowl for leftover yumminess. Granddaddy always got the first and second piece. After that, we could get a slice. It was heaven in our mouth. We'd get a gallon of French vanilla ice cream every week to have with the cake. I bake a little now but have never been able to do what she did."

"I look back now and wonder how a woman with such a sour disposition could make something so sweet. Knowing what I know about life, I've learned that maybe that was her way to show love. People can only give you what they have. If you don't get anything else from me, get that. It will save you a lot of heartache and time."

"Granddaddy used to tell a story about grandma that I remember to this day. It perfectly describes what she was like and what it could be like to live with her. He said that one day, Grandma was going on and on nagging about something and it was too much for him. She was biting his head off, so he went and sat on the porch to get away. The mosquitos were bad, and they were biting too. He couldn't get any peace there either and he had to decide which was worse, putting up with one nagging wife inside or a thousand nagging mosquitos outside. He opted to stay outside. I know, it's hilarious. I never tire of thinking about that story."

"Our daughter, Rashidah, is one of the most loving beings on the planet and she is very much like her great-grandmother. She does not play. She is a stickler for decency and things being in order. She will tell you exactly what she thinks even if you didn't ask and what you're not going to do is get on her nerves. She has no time for that. I can't wait for the two of you to get to know each other. You'll love her. She is my biggest cheerleader and sometimes she thinks she is the mother."

"Actually both of the children, Rashidah and Ajamou, are protectors and watchers over me. I think sometimes they worry too much, but it is part of their showing love. One day they will tell their grandchildren stories about me that they remember. Memories are like candles on a cake, they come together as reminders of where we've been and illuminate where we're going. I think that even though we can't predict the future or see into it, our memories, life lessons, and stories from our past are like the fireflies we used to catch down south."

"They provide a flash of light that can help us see our way making sure we're going in the right direction as we age. That might not make sense to some but to me those memories, lessons, and stories have travelled with me and made my journey easier by giving me a peek at who and where I've been and clues to who I'll be and where I'll go."

"Grandma had the most beautiful skin, just a shade or two lighter than Rashidah. Her hair was so shiny when I was young. She'd sometimes let me brush it for her. When she got older, her mind and her health declined. She was in hospice care a couple of times but her will was strong in her spirit, even though her body didn't agree. She lived years after they said she wouldn't."

"I went to see her a couple of times when I visited Mama. We'd go to the nursing home together. Mama had to put her there because it got too hard to care for her at home and she would sometimes get agitated and combative. But Mama went daily without fail. She washed her clothes even though they had a laundry service. She fed her, cleaned her, combed her hair and would talk to her even though eventually, Grandma didn't say much at all."

"Her decline was sad to watch. She went from being a cannon to a firecracker and then to a wooden stick match whose flame would quickly extinguish once it was lit. The last couple of times I saw her, she thought I was her youngest daughter, the one I stayed with when I moved to Milwaukee. At first, I would try to correct her, but it became clear that she didn't understand so I went with it. I can still remember the last time I saw her."

"I combed her hair, which was now so long, but not as shiny or thick. I took my time and her demeanor said she enjoyed it. Maybe like me, for a moment, she remembered that feeling from years ago and was transported back."

"I miss her. When I got the call that she passed, I wanted to come home, but my mother insisted that I not. She said she wanted me to remember my grandma the way she was. Even still, I wanted to support my mom in her time of loss. I realized that maybe to her, she'd lost her mom years ago, and this was all just a formality. I honored her wish. I have to trust that my grandma knew we loved her."

"Our granddaddy died years earlier after developing Black Lung Disease from working in the coal mines. He was also diabetic and had a leg amputated because of that. He never fully recovered from that. That scared me because I thought of him as larger than life, but in the end, life brought about his death. We, you and I, didn't go to his funeral either, but at that time, we were in the street, hustling in South Carolina and Atlanta, and deep in our addiction."

"Yes, Sis, they are tears. It makes me sad to think about our grandparents. I owe them so much and I'd like to think that even though we took a different path than they wanted, that they'd both be proud of us now. All in all, we did not have a bad childhood. We had our parents and even after the divorce, we spent time with them both. We went to private and public school and had a church-going family. We never missed a meal. We ate a lot of chili and spaghetti, but we were never hungry. Those were quick, easy, filling meals. They weren't expensive and mom worked a lot."

"I don't ever remember her not working, do you? She worked in the school system in the office, and she was the first Black woman to become an officer on the force at the local university. She wasn't a bad mother. She kept us fed, clothed, and educated. She even sewed for us. She taught us about God and made us do chores. She encouraged our friendships and all of our friends adored her. I find that interesting because all of our children's friends adore us."

"We know that she loved us, but she was not the warm, fuzzy type. I'm not sure why. Her mother wasn't that type either. Maybe that trait is handed down. But, then again, we are the warm, fuzzy type. So, I don't know. I always felt that Mama loved us out of duty. Maybe we are the way we are because we didn't get that warm, fuzzy feeling, and internally we knew the importance of it. So, we made sure to incorporate that in all of our relationships."

"I remember when the children were born. Yes, Rashidah and Ajamou, you got it. Anyway, I've always been somewhat warm and fuzzy, but after they were born, I made a very conscious decision to be a huggy, touchy and welcoming mom to the kids. That is exactly what we have become. We are known for our hugs. One of our community daughters recently said that a hug from me is like an answered prayer. My God what a statement that was. I know I'm emotional, some would say too emotional, but her saying that made me cry. Why? Because I knew that I was giving what I wanted to give, and that people were getting what I wanted them to get."

"I've always believed in gifts from God and have wanted the gift of laying on hands. I don't mean I touch someone, they become unconscious, and when they wake up their cancer is healed, or they were blind and could now see. What I've wanted is to hug people and have them feel the love. I want them to feel lifted and encouraged. I want them to get that hug and use it as a vehicle to drive away stress, negativity, or sadness and take in love. Just love. Even for a few minutes that can make such a difference to someone. It can be what they need to feel a little better and go a little further."

"Love is an action word and hugging is an action. Therefore in my opinion, it is love. Some are not comfortable with hugs and in that case, a touch on the shoulder or the back can generate the same feeling. When I sense that touch can't be used, I give eye contact, a kind word, a small gesture. It's all love in its many forms of display."

"It is important to me that you believe and understand, maybe because then I'll more firmly believe and understand that nobody specific is to blame for our life, the things we went through, or the decisions we made. But I also believe that we, you and I, have to take responsibility for those decisions in order to reverse the outcome, or at least try to turn right side up what we've turned upside down. Trust that after I left you, my bad decision-making didn't end. I made more. Many, many more. Our experiences in the past have an influence over our present-day decisions."

"I admit I kept you hostage in the past, but in doing so I've saved you from some real unpleasantness that occurred because of my decisions. Now that you're free, I can tell you that I'm sure that we will make more decisions that might not be the best. I do think that we've grown a lot, learned a lot, and that the bad decisions we make in the future will not be as bad or have the level of consequences of the bad decisions we made in the past."

"When you know better, you do better. Does that make sense to you? Good. That makes me happy, because I can't promise you that things will be perfect now that you've been released. What I promise you is that I'm strong now. I'm not as strong as I want to be, but I'm strong enough to hold you up with one arm and continue training to get stronger with the other. I've trained and fought hard for this day. I know you think I left you, and I did. But you need to know that I had nothing positive, nothing sure to offer you then. Had I not taken my time to get better we might have both perished."

"It was almost like being on an airplane that crashed and putting the oxygen mask on myself before trying to save you. You needed a life transplant and for over 30 years, I was not a suitable donor. Even though we are one and the same, somehow, I feel responsible for you. Maybe I thought I was the stronger half and that I could endure more. I wanted to be able to let you rest, heal, recover, restore, and rebuild. I just didn't think it would take me so long to create a space for you to do that."

"We are like twins. One is stronger where one may be weaker and vice versa. It is certainly no disrespect to you. Sis, you always carried your weight as best you could. When I was low on self-esteem, energy, or the desire to live another day, you willingly gave to me from your supply and I took. I tried to do the same for you. I guess like many relationships ours was codependent."

"I think we survived by taking turns when it came to accepting our reality. When we could no longer do it, we'd tap out so the other could jump in. When I cowered on the floor in the corner, licking the wounds inflicted by another with the toe and heel of a boot, you were there to carry on. You had what it took for us to get up, cover any obvious bruises, find an outfit and hit the street to get paid or face more of the same."

"Do you remember when we were 15, and we took all the meds we could sneak out of the house. We got some blackberry wine from the liquor store that didn't card us because we looked older and flirted with the clerk. Yes, that's right, we had stolen Granddaddy's key to the church and went in the basement, either to take our life or pray not to take our life. We swallowed the pills with the wine and waited. We got ill but not ill enough."

"I remember feeling scared that if we died, we'd go to hell because that's what we were taught. I threw up and felt faint. I can't remember between that and an ambulance, the hospital, guilt, shame, and embarrassment. Do you remember? Did we go to the phone and call for help? Did help show up because they had a need to come to church? I'm sure we were told but I blocked it out. Apparently you did too."

"I don't remember much of those days in the hospital except feeling sick and full of shame, having to talk to all kinds of people and having nothing to say, and being told constantly that we had to get out of bed. Yes, I do remember the look in Mama's eyes as we did our best to avoid eye contact. We begged her to let us stay with Daddy down south because the look in her eyes couldn't be avoided forever. She was so confused and humiliated by what happened, that once Daddy said he would be glad for us to come, she quickly consented."

"Wow, though, look at where we came from. We went from wanting to die to fighting to live. I get very teary-eyed thinking about that. I wonder how many people that I come across in a day have been or are in that same position. If we had known then what we know now, things would be different. But we had to go through that process. That process made us who we are. Better, stronger, wiser, more resilient women. Now that I've pulled you out, I hope that we can use our combined energy to pull other women out of that place where they've been stuck."

"Girl, where was our mind back then? What was making our life so chaotic? Yes, we really started acting up and acting out. We were already on the path to self-destruction, going headfirst downhill at 190 miles an hour with no seatbelt, helmet or brakes. Whatever we crashed into; it wasn't going to end well for us."

"Do you remember the older man we met at church? Yes, that's right, his name was Michael. I say older, and I mean that he was a grown man, not a senior citizen. We weren't yet grown. We started spending time with him and a couple other military men at the barracks on the base. Michael was married and away from home. He was one of but not the first."

"That title belongs to a man who was visiting here from Africa. We met him through someone else that we had no business knowing. We ended up at his apartment one day. We were a virgin when we arrived but not when we left. Once we realized what was happening and his intentions, we pleaded with him, telling him 'no' several times. We tried pushing him away and he responded by saying it wouldn't hurt. He covered our mouth with his hand and our body with his body, which felt like ten times our weight. We were unable to resist. The pain shot through us and we were forever changed."

"I look back at that part of our life and I still ask myself how we ended up there. Were we looking for love, acceptance, escape, control? Or were we just hot and young? I've uncovered many things about us on my journey, but still no feasible answer for that. I wonder how deep I have to go to get the answer and how much more work has to be done to uncover it."

"Of course, there are always the other questions. Do I really want to know? What do I do with the information once I have it? Were we touched inappropriately as a child? Did we have a tremendously low level of self-esteem? No, I've never gone to traditional therapy although I've thought about it. I've seen a counselor and at one time was seeing a life coach for other reasons. My life coach helped me work through some things. I'm considering going back."

"Maybe we wanted to be grown, to get out of Mama's house. I tend to believe all of the possible answers at different times. How about you? What do you think? Ok, I see we are in agreement in our confusion. Over the years, my portion of our mind has become so muddled and some things I've strived to forget won't leave while others disappear as if they never happened. On the other hand, at least some of the things that I want to hold onto become void of specific details, and I struggle to hold on to the remnants. I pray daily hoping that other memories were a bad dream, only to realize they are real. Does that make sense to you? Funny how that works."

"The mind can either be a steel strap holding a memory captive until it slowly dies or it can be a sieve, releasing the painful memory quickly down the drain to a place it can't come back from. Unfortunately, there are also pleasant memories that get mixed in with the others and fall through the sieve as well. I find myself trying to separate the memories, holding onto some while almost pushing the others away."

"What? What did you say? I'm sorry for talking over you. Your voice, for lack of use over the decades, is quiet. It is still trying to find strength and volume. Even at its loudest, I don't think your voice could compare to mine. I think all of our life, I've been louder than you and once I left you behind, I got even louder."

"You see, I had to speak for myself in my obvious presence and for you in your quiet absence. I had to yell so they'd know I meant business, and that I wasn't having it anymore. Sometimes, that force was to draw attention, other times, admittedly, it was to cause intimidation or at least make people wonder how to take me or how to proceed. Something just came to mind. The only time I was quiet, the only time I whimpered or whispered, was when the attacks I suffered were physical. My God. The only times I barely uttered a sound was when I had to prove what a bad bitch I was and that I could take it."

"I knew during those times that to yell, scream, or cry out would only make me look weak and increase the intensity and duration of what I was already being made to endure. It almost at times seemed like a sick game. Would I cry or scream at a bloody nose? Would it take a bloody nose, a bloody lip, and ringing in the ears? How many lashes from a wire hanger would produce more than silent tears? How many would produce a cry, a pleading, or a bloody lip caused by me biting down on my own lip – causing more pain just to not acknowledge the initial pain. It is crazy when I look back. Help us Father."

"Together Sis, you and I were not strong enough to fight it, to fight against it. I guess our strength came from the fact that we could take it, each and every time. What does that say when a woman will take that level of treatment in silence but will raise the roof if someone is late for family dinner? One of our community daughters is known for saying 'look out y'all, she's going to blow' whenever she knows I'm about to go off. Honestly, to take such abuse as if it is a requirement for taking up space on this earth is a form of insanity."

"Oh, your question, I almost forgot. You asked what memories I wish would disappear and what memories am I desperately trying to hold onto. That question is a whole conversation in itself. What do I want to let go of but can't?"

¶ "I want to let go of just turning eighteen and standing on a corner in Columbia, South Carolina in broad daylight and being slapped across my face. It was one firm slap that turned my head. The shock and embarrassment were almost more intense than the slap itself. In our insanity, we felt offended that we were subjected to this in public in the light of day as if it was wrong then and there, but perfectly acceptable behind closed doors."

"Being subjected to that in public, I wanted to strangle him that very night in his sleep. After that, my confused mental state got even more twisted and I believed it was okay for him to hit, punch, kick me, spit on me, and curse at me at any time and any place. What had been done in the private dark had now come into the public light. Help us Father. Even now, the memory of that day makes me lower my eyes with shame and I can feel my heart race in fear, even though I know it's just a memory and I'm safe here with you."

"I want to let go of almost a week that I spent in that nasty Charleston County Jail going through cocaine and heroin withdrawal because of a prostitution charge. Nobody can convince me that there isn't a God. That was a terrible time of diarrhea in unclean conditions, toilet paper that felt like sandpaper, food with a smell that made me vomit more than withdrawal, and a fear of showering. The little sleep I did have was burdened by bad dreams, and I didn't have any hope of anything much better than what I currently had."

"If it's true that God hears our every request, I wore his name out. I went between God please help me to live and God please just take my life. Either way I begged for more than I felt I was worthy of. I promised that if I got out of there I'd never use again or turn another trick. I know you know that once I got out, I got high then cleaned myself up. Important things first. After that, I went about trying to get back to work. There was money to be made and I was reminded in a not nice way how much I'd missed out on and how my dumb ass was responsible for getting popped by the cops."

"I'd like to let go of the memory of sitting in an official room talking about living with Mama or Daddy, two people that we adored. Even as a child, I knew we would be the product of a broken home. For some reason, the word *broken* always stuck with me. I'd like to let go of looking at our children for 30 years wondering what the other two would have looked like. The one we tried to keep and lost through miscarriage and the one we decided to abort."

"Help me Father. Protect me from the memories that threaten to drive me mad. I always blamed myself for the miscarriage, but as I've aged and learned more, I realize that maybe it wasn't all my fault. However, the child I aborted is my fault. I made that decision, even though I might have had other options. I've always been sure that if anything I've ever done would send me to hell, it would be that. Whether or not it does, I feel like I've lived in hell on Earth since that day."

"I just recently confessed that act to our children. Both of them were so understanding that it brought tears to my eyes. Our son said that is not what hurt him.

What hurt him is that I carried that shame and guilt for almost 30 years. The wisdom of the youth. I've asked God for forgiveness countless times and I have to believe he has granted it. Honestly, I struggled to forgive myself. Shit, at the time Sis, there were days where I fought to hold on to my sanity and my own life. I was in the church basement all over again."

"I never thought I'd have this conversation with you, and I'm asking you for forgiveness and understanding as well. The ironic thing is that I'm a better than good mom, a bonus mom, and a village mom. I'm a work mom and I'm nurturing to all. If I was a nursery rhyme, I'd be the old woman in the shoe who had so many children she didn't know what to do. I've wondered if God gave us the spirit of nurturing to tell us that not only does he forgive us, but that he trusts us to love and to be maternal to so many."

"I am human and sometimes the human side comes out and I want to exert myself. But for the most part, I love without judgment and I love because of, not in spite of. What? Would I do it again? You mean have an abortion? Knowing what I know now, no, I don't think I would. Young and not so young women and men have come to me on multiple occasions to ask for counsel on that matter. I listen and give as honest of a response as I can. Each of us must do what is best for us in our circumstance and be willing to accept the consequences and to pray. Always pray for guidance. It's a decision we can't undo."

"You and I are a source of love and healing and people feel comfortable talking to us about things. I'm usually okay with most subjects but that still makes me feel a certain way inside. No, I didn't tell the father. He was married. Unhappy, but still married and had made it way too clear to me that he didn't want any more children. All I can do at this point is believe that God has forgiven me, continue to forgive myself, be grateful for the understanding of our children, hope that the child's father would forgive me, and pray that the child that still lives in a corner of my heart would forgive me. Enough of that."

"Know that, even that thing we try to destroy in our life, God can give us back a thousand times. I know because for us it was children to love. That very act is how I know that not only is restoration possible, but often probable with faith, work, and the hand of God."

"Okay where was I? That's right, memories I'd like to forget. A few more. The first time I used cocaine and heroin, the first time I traded sex for money, making the decision to drop out of high school, and marrying a man I barely knew are just some. On the other end, there are memories I hope I hold on to forever. I know I'm all over the place. Stop me if I go too fast or if you have a question or something to add. Life doesn't happen in bullet points. It's more like a road map, which sometimes requires detours, including going back to start over."

"We are born, and we die. What happens in between follows no specific order or path. Some graduate, get married, have children and buy a home. Others never graduate or marry, have children, buy a home and then decided to go back at a later time to graduate. You would understand that if I'd come back for you sooner so you could live this life with me, and travel the journey I've been on since we parted."

"The memories I want to hold are many because life has by no means been all tragedy and trauma. I want to remember things like the day each grandchild was born. I was there. I wish you could have been there, too. Each one was so perfect, each a different shade of Black beauty. I will also remember the day the children that are mine were born. I was more relieved than anything. I was so afraid that the years of abuse to my body from drugs and sex work would cause them to have a deficiency or abnormality of some kind. I'd have loved them anyway, but the world can be cruel. I swear when they were born, I looked at them and knew the face of God. The difference with the grands is that they came from what came from me. I knew then that even when I was no longer here, I'd live forever."

"I want to remember driving our daughter to Texas to take a teaching position for a couple of years. We'd never been separated for more than a few days. Child, I can't tell you how much my heart wept. It was a hell of a trip. I hit a deer on the way. It was his fault. He ran in front of me. He was stunned for a minute but got up and took off. I wanted to go find him, but it was almost dark and nobody else was too concerned. I wanted to keep driving but my family said no and relieved me of my duties. We got there, spent the night and made sure she was good before driving back to Milwaukee. By the time we got back, I don't think I ever felt so tired and alone in my life."

"I want to remember the day our son was asked to be a keynote speaker at a university he flunked out of earlier in his life. I want to remember the first Heal the Hood block party. Ajamou wanted to make a difference and his vision took off. Several amazing things have sprung from his vision. I want to remember every time I took an HIV test that came back negative, because I know the life we used to live."

"I want to remember every Sunday night when I'd make nachos and popcorn, and the kids and I would watch America's Funniest Home Videos. Then we'd watch the same movies over and over as if we'd never seen them before, yet we knew every line. I don't know if they realized how little money I had to take care of us. If love, adventures, and laughs were any indicator, I guess we had all we needed."

"I hold tightly to seeing them both graduate high school because I never did. I hold on to taking their pictures before prom. We never went. I look back and smile still at catching the lightening bugs in a jar. I remember when we used to sing in the church choir. I didn't particularly care for church as a child, but being in the choir always made me happy. I want to remember each time I fell in love, even if it didn't always end the way I wanted it to. Standing on a ship in the middle of the ocean looking at the sunrise over the water is a scene and a feeling I want to always remember. It was my first, and thus far, my only cruise."

"After I left you there were so many beautiful memories I wish you could have shared with me. I can't tell you how the guilt of leaving you sometimes paralyzed me. I promised myself that once I got straight, I mean really straight, that I would come back for you. I wanted to come back at a time when I had it all together, a time when I could make you proud of us. The truth is, I'd probably have gotten better and stronger quicker if you were by my side, instead of trying to do it alone. I wanted to be strong enough to help you get over the trauma that I'm still healing from, because it is truly a work in progress."

"I don't know exactly how long it has taken to get to this point, I just know that one day I started. I started being able to face the monsters that hid under the bed, in my closet, and in the corners of my mind. I would make a bit of progress, think I was better, and then the nightmares would be back. Or out of the blue, I'd remember getting high, swallowing and tasting that getting high taste. And all the progress I made would digress."

"One day I could look in the mirror, brush my teeth, and have a pleasant thought, but that night, I'd wake up with a pillow stained with a corrosive combination of tears and sweat. God knows if I could tell you when the magic moment of healing takes place I would, because to the degree that I'm healed, I want you healed also. I wish I could give you a countdown. Sometimes I wonder if life is a continuous rollercoaster of hurt, heal, breathe, and repeat."

"I think that healing is like running a marathon. It has to be done in sections; it's easier to conquer it that way. When I think about it, I can't see the finish line, but I believe that each hurdle, each mile, each obstacle is a finish line by itself. Completing those should be celebrated because it matters. It counts and without conquering each mile, each fear, each failure, trauma, and loss, we will never make it to the place where we are unburdened. The place where we can cross the finish line, going from victim to victorious. Sometimes you have to break it down to carry the weight of it all, piece by piece."

"It's like recovery, Sis. One day at a time and when needed, one hour or one minute at a time. It has only been in recent years that I've been able to have a conversation with myself, let alone anyone else, including you. A conversation that was raw, uncut, unfiltered. The truth and nothing but the truth. Once I was willing to talk about it in my head, no voice, only silent words, I knew I was on the right track."

"Next, I added the words out loud, just a few at a time. I needed time to get to a place of comfort with those words. I would speak them out loud in the dark and then I began to tell people I trusted, just one or two. My comfort level increased. I knew that one day I could confront you, not right away, but one day."

"Well, I guess that day has come. What? No, not everyone was receptive to our transparency. Looking back now, the ones with the most problems were men. One that I was in a relationship with told me that although he was okay with my past, he didn't want me bringing it up to his family or anyone he knows, because he didn't want them to think that he would be with that kind of woman. I was crushed because I was not that kind of woman and he wasn't willing to publicly defend me and my transformation. He was much more concerned with what people would think. Those types of incidents would occasionally make me go back in the corner to lick my wounds and get the strength to try again."

"Do you remember our move to South Carolina? Have we talked about it since you stepped out of the past? How far back in Charleston do you want us to go? This doesn't happen to me often but talking to you makes me a little nervous. I'm usually comfortable talking to corporate heads or crack heads, presidents or prostitutes. But for some reason, you slightly unnerve me, so I know I'm rambling on and on. I'm probably repeating things but I don't want to leave anything out. I want us to share every old memory that you have and every new memory that I have, new to you, but not to me. I've been collecting memories without you since I stepped off that Greyhound bus in Milwaukee on August 8, 1985."

"Mom's birthday. I never thought about it before, but what a gift for her to have her daughter closer to home, not using drugs or being an evening hostess, but staying with her sister and her husband, who, it seemed to me, went to church every day of the week. That's an exaggeration, but not by much. I hadn't been in a church since the day I went in with Blackberry liquor. So when my aunt and her husband went, I went. I felt so out of place, like the church would burn down once my presence was detected."

"Girl, when they put me on that bus, my plan was to come back after six months of getting my life together. I got on the bus with no money. An addict on the road with money is a dangerous thing. It's a sure setup for getting off at the next stop to go in search of a high. I had some food and something to drink. I remember like it was yesterday, even though this past August made thirty-four years. I only had a few belongings because I'd run away from all I had – clothes, shoes, jewelry and personal items. Those thing don't mean much to me, even to this day. I've gone through the cycle too many times. I'd left what I knew, hoping and praying that I was headed towards something better."

"The reality is that anything would have been better. There I go again, skipping ahead in the story. It could be nerves or confirmation that life often goes forward then backwards, in circles, takes detours, climbs mountain, and falls of cliffs. So, I was asking if you remembered our move to Charleston. I'm sure that by the time we got there we were already bent. Not broken, but bent. We were 15 or 16-years-old. We didn't know if Charleston was ready for us, but looking back, we sure weren't ready for Charleston."

"In some ways, it was a lose-lose situation. We got tested and enrolled in high school. The curriculum was different, and it lacked the ability to hold my interest and focus. I felt out of place there. Of course, I remember feeling out of place before we left. What's even more interesting is that sometimes I still feel out of place, but as a testament to our growth, we don't feel that way as much. I wonder if now that you're free, you'll feel the same way."

"Anyway, even though we were born there, we had no southern accent. We left as a baby and traveled a bit as military minors. Most of our childhood was primarily spent in frigid Minnesota, and because of Mama's insistence that we speak proper English, we had a different accent than the people of Charleston. I'll admit there is something so hospitable in that southern drawl, though."

"Even though we are devoid of the southern accent and after decades of being out of the south, I still pride myself on being a southern woman at heart. Whether in terms of a stereotype or my own perception, I know I'm a southern woman because I like the feel of the ground under my feet. No shoes, just the soil on my skin. I like the doors and windows open inviting the light and most who desire to enter. I don't know how to cook for a couple of people, so there is always food going out. I like to sit on the porch fighting off some insects while marveling at the beauty of others that create flickering lights in the sky or hover above the flowers in my yard, drawing my eyes to every color and blossom."

"I don't know. There's just something about the holistic, natural riches of the south that makes a southern woman special. I always thank Daddy's sisters for that. Looking back, I remember certain things I saw them do that I do now, and when I imitate them my spirit smiles."

"The weather in the south, now that held our interest. It was beautiful most of the time. Charleston sits on the edge of the water. I love water. We'd go catch crabs and have crab boils at daddy's house. And the gardens. Looking at them was almost sensory overload. To me, they were comparable to the gardens I saw in Hawaii and Jamaica."

"The south grows lots of beautiful things, including Black men. Baby, the men! We were really still just a girl. Shapely, curious, fast-thinking and fast-acting, but still a girl. We had an eye for the men, and they had an eye for us. We met a friend of daddy's that had a brother who had an eye for us. At that point, Daddy was eager to keep us around and therefore, he figured it was okay to give in to me when I made it clear that we wanted to date."

"We ended up in a relationship that progressed too quickly to moving in together. The entire duration of that, you and I were in high school. Do you remember? He worked during the day while we went to school and at night, we played house. We would visit Daddy and then visit his family, like we were a normal, grown ass couple. The reality that I can admit today is that, it was becoming a bit of a bore. I was bored with school and playing house. My mister was talking marriage once I turned of age. I knew then, and you probably did too, that the whole scene was crazy and we had to be crazy as well to even entertain the thought."

"So, another chapter of our life began. While out in the neighborhood, headed to a local ice cream parlor, we met the next *him*, the preacher's kid. He was the *him* that would prove to us that we weren't as grown as we thought we were, and we really weren't running anything but our mouth and our life into the ground."

"No, we don't say his name. He is like the Candyman. If his name is said too many times, he may appear in the very mirror you just came out of. So, to be on the safe side, he is referred to as the preacher's kid. His father was a preacher who also had an eye for me, and made sure that I knew."

"Anyway, we met him during our walk, and he struck up a conversation. We never went back to our play husband after that, except to grab some stuff while he wasn't there. We also never went back to school. Do you remember we hid at Preacher Kid's house? Although we didn't call it that"

"Play Husband and Daddy joined forces around the neighborhood looking for us. They passed flyers with our photo. At one time, Play Husband, or Larry, even knocked on our new door because someone in the area said they thought they saw us there. We stayed in for quite a while, then one day, Preacher's Kid came home and said we were moving to a new place where I would be safe. No bigger lie has ever been told."

"We moved, got new clothes, and set up a new identity. New name, new wigs, new life. To this day, I can't remember the exact conversation, but he convinced us that we didn't have to live like we had been, and that he could help us make the kind of money we needed to sustain the life we wanted. We were intrigued and the lessons started. Shit, we were doing it anyway and we agreed with him, we might as well get paid to do it."

"I don't know about you, but I didn't feel as bad as I should have for pulling a disappearing act on our former life. We left behind our life as a straight-A student in senior year. Mama's long-time partner promised to pay for our entire college education, and he could afford it. The plan was to graduate from high school, attend college and study police science, and then go to law school to become an attorney. Instead, we got involved in a life where we tried avoiding then police, ended up getting arrested by them, and needing our own fucking lawyer."

"Life is a bitch, but at some point, you just hope to get it right. Preacher's Kid watched us, coached us, and gave us life-saving tips. You would have thought that was an indicator of what we were in for, but we were oblivious. I remember like it was yesterday – the first time, the first trick we turned. We earned a fifty-dollar bill for less than ten minutes of what we didn't even consider work. From there it was all uphill and downhill at the same time."

"We didn't stay in Charleston long because I still wasn't 18 and therefore only worked under the cover of night. Soon, we moved from Charleston to Columbia because nobody would look for us there. We needed to be able to live as safely as possible with an unsafe lifestyle. Thinking about that today sounds crazy as shit. Our skills, along with our client base and daily income grew."

"Do you remember the first time we got high? I'm sure we can both agree that the experience was another beginning of another end. Yes, that's right. We were 17 years old. We knew nothing of hardcore drugs, although, by that time, we knew how to function with plenty of alcohol in our system and a weed high. Even with those experiences, we were not at all prepared for the dark, demonic world of speedball – cocaine and heroin combined."

"Thank you God for your presence in that time for saving a life we did everything to take. The cocaine took us up and the heroin brought us down. The feeling was foreign at first, but not too foreign that we didn't do it every day for 5 or 6 years, at least two times a day, and most often at its heaviest, three times a day. The cost was ridiculous. Remember, it wasn't just us, but him, too. The cost was astronomical, but when you made money the way that we did, it seemed like chump change. The coins came steadily, and the tricks turned regularly."

"We were different. We were not the usual bitch on the block. We were a new commodity in that area. To keep it real, we weren't just good because of the product, but because of our personality. Granted, we were the bomb sexually, but our demeanor, our conversation and our natural charm made our tricks feel like they weren't just picking up paid-for-pussy, but were picking up someone they might actually deal with in real life. The mind can believe what we tell it to believe. I was someone who made them feel more like friends than freaks."

"We took an odd pride in what we did because even then, we were people pleasers and would often get clients who wanted to talk to us about things they couldn't or didn't feel comfortable talking about at home or to anyone else. I think that our self-esteem was so low and our self-love so non-existent that once we found out that men and the occasional woman or couples would pay to be in our presence, we got a false sense of value and self-worth, of control."

"We assessed our value with dollar amounts and those we regularly did business with kept weekly appointments, paid the asking price, and tipped well. It got to the point where a few were even extended a line of credit with a more than reasonable interest rate. It was never a problem to collect on that debt. We got more and more comfortable with what we were doing or rather we grew numb to it. Occasionally, we'd mentally check out and forget one of the rules. We just felt like all the bad things that could happen to us wouldn't happen, as if what was happening wasn't bad enough."

"I remember the day we jumped in a car after making a deal and we didn't look in the backseat. Our dumb ass paid the price for that mistake. As we gave the driver directions to the motel room, a second man popped up from behind my seat and put a gun to the back of my head. They both laughed, calling me names and telling me they weren't going to pay for shit, but they would have what they wanted for as long as they wanted it. You and I were more scared of what the preacher's kid was going to do to us if and when we got back. We'd be punished once for wasting time, twice for being stupid and not following the correct procedure, and three times for allowing some trick to get free product."

"They couldn't do anything worse to us except kill us and maybe, just maybe, that would be better. Those men were rapists and kidnappers, but they were honest because they did what they said they would. They drove to a secluded area, pulled over, shut off the engine, and pulled us out. With the gun pointed at us constantly, they made us undress completely. We kept our eyes on the gun wondering if it was even loaded, but not wanting to suffer the fate of finding out."

"Even when we tasted blood at the corner of our mouth from the slap we received for moving too slow, we still kept our eyes trained on the gun. The only time we couldn't see the gun was when we were forced to lay down on the ground and open our legs. We could feel the barrel go inside us and knew it was still present."

"You're crying as if you remember. There is no need to apologize at all. I've shed a million tears over that night. Yes, you're right. One kept the gun inside us and then ran it along our legs while the other straddled us, forcing himself in our mouth, telling us that we knew what to do. So we did exactly that. He pulled out of our mouth and finished all over our face, rubbing it in."

"They took turns raping us until they got tired of us. Then they told us to dress quickly. They put us back in the car and had the sick decency to push us out across the street from where they picked us up. No, it's not a nightmare because we both remember each detail the same. Yep, we threw up on the corner and with weak knees, headed to the hotel, knowing what would be waiting for us."

"I sometimes see those things we endured happening to other people and I think that there is no way that we survived, but we did, Sis. We did. We were right about what was waiting on us, though. We ran into the preacher's kid on the way to the hotel. We had not checked in or turned a trick, so he came looking for us. He knew right away that something had happened. Before we could get the story out, the slap came, and he escorted us the few blocks to the hotel. The whole time, he told us what fate awaited us and why."

"I felt like someone on death row being escorted to the gas chamber. We survived the ordeal and the punishment. We thought it was good luck, but there isn't that much luck in the world. It was God. It was God that day and it was God the day we were again forced at gun point to give oral sex to a trick who kept telling us how dirty we were and how we break up homes. It was God the day we accidentally knocked over the cup that contained our cooked dope and the preacher's kid went ballistic on us."

"It was God who kept us when we started selling the dope and charged people to get high in the other room. Remember that white girl? I know you do because I'll never forget her. She took too big of a shot and fell out. She was breathing but we couldn't get her to come to. I wanted to call 911 but of course we couldn't. So we and the preacher's kid carried her out back by the railroad tracks. Several hookers had recently been murdered and found along that stretch, but nobody really cared. We didn't matter. We never heard about her or saw her again for that matter. We moved into another motel for a while. I'd like to think she regained consciousness and somehow got away and got help."

"You and I didn't realize it during those years, but we saw evidence of God daily. God kept us as we worked. He kept us when we ran away, even the time we had no money and had to sleep on a urine-soaked concrete slab between two buildings across from the Greyhound station. We did that for two days, and snuck out to turn tricks in the car. We lowered prices because we needed to get high and try to buy a ticket to anywhere, because anywhere was better than where we were."

"We were half crazy those days, not clean and had gone from charging triple digits per hour to 'give me whatever you got' just to survive. We took a chance and went to wash up as best we could at the bus station bathroom and when we came outside, we saw Preacher's Kid standing in front of that burgundy Chrysler he drove. I'm convinced to this day that someone saw us in the area and tipped him off."

"It was like a scene from a movie. He opened the car door without saying a word and we got in. This time we were being driven to our execution, instead of walking. He didn't need to speak because what is understood doesn't need to be said. We were beaten and belittled and actually could not walk for a couple of days because of bruising and swelling. There is only so much covering up one can do with makeup or clothes."

"He wanted to have sex with us afterwards because he knew we'd be in for a couple of days. He claimed we were better when we weren't getting used up all the time. Although we had some insane love for him, or some insane something, we did not want him. We didn't want to be touched. It hurt, so we did what we often did, tuned out to his touch and words and saved the tears for the shower."

"I want you to know that after having sex on demand for years, we did end up having a normal sex life, as normal as possible in our case. Like most people, we are aware of what we do and don't like, which is nice because at one time, what we liked was to be paid. I think I'm more critical of men than I'd otherwise be, simply because I've seen them in a different way, through a different lens."

"I suppose the men we dealt with are like many others, they were willing to pay to turn their fantasies to realities, even if just for a few minutes. When it comes to the fantasy and fetish, I always wondered what happened in a man's life that made him want to be with a woman he can call mommy, and ask that woman to spank him because he's been bad."

"I know girl, me too. I'd love to un-see some of the things we've seen. We wondered why a guy who seemed nice and respectable would pay good money to have a woman stick a bobby pin in and out of his belly button so he could get an erection and have an orgasm. What the hell was he doing when he figured out he liked that? That's right, he never wanted anything else. We stayed fully clothed when we did that, at his request. I don't know. I wondered, but never enough to dare ask. I didn't want to run away a client and the answer may have caused even more questions. Each to his or her own."

"Once I left the life, I started thinking about our own truths in sexuality and how comfortable we were with them, or even sharing them. We are good now, but it was a process like everything else. As I've aged, I notice that a great deal of women are not comfortable with their sexuality, let alone comfortable talking about it. It's so sad that many women are uncomfortable with something so natural. They don't explore it, and they allow others to put them in a box or they choose to act like they are everything else but a sexual being."

"When we are not honest with self, we can't be honest with our partners. There are women who do not regularly masturbate but look down on women who do. I do not think that self-service is a replacement for a relationship, and we should be clear about that. However, I also don't think it's the worst thing in the world to have a battery-operated companion, a box of batteries, and a vivid imagination. Those who haven't tried it shouldn't knock it, and those who try it or regularly practice it have to decide the course for them."

Part Four

Milwaukee Memoirs

"We were picked up at the bus station by our aunt and uncle. As I'm sure I said earlier, our intention was to stay in Milwaukee for about six months to get clean. I'd have gone straight to the dope man if I knew where he was when I got off that bus, so I knew I had some work to do. I knew it would take time. We had escaped the place and the people, but we hadn't escaped self. Wherever you go, there you are. We hadn't escaped the craving, the desperate need to get high."

"God Help Me became my mantra. Damn a day at a time. I was operating on a minute at a time intervals. My mouth would water at the thought. My pulse would race. I could almost smell it in the air. I was actually glad that you weren't with me at that time. It was enough of a struggle just to keep my sanity; I don't think I could have helped you at all."

"I didn't know what to do. I didn't fit in. I was a fish out of water. Talk about moving from one extreme to another. We went from being in the streets tricking daily and getting high to going to church for Sunday service, morning and evening, bible study, prayer meeting and any other occasion in the week. I thought the church would burn down every time I walked in, that or I'd spontaneously combust. I felt like I couldn't breathe. That all changed as I developed an instant relationship with a man."

"We met our children's father soon after coming to Milwaukee. His friend lived next door to my aunt and uncle. He was helping with some exterior painting. I saw him across the fence, and we struck up a conversation. The first time we talked, I'm sure he painted that window trim 20 times. I like your laugh, but girl its true. He kept talking, dipping that brush in the paint can, and painting that window trim."

"We went out to dinner and before you know it, we were spending all of our time together, whenever we could. Looking back, it would have been better for me to spend time working on myself. I was distracted from the reason I was here, so it took much longer to deal with my issues. I was trying to learn his way of life, which was totally different from mine, but God knows I suffered in silence. I was trying to go straight but was dealing with the residuals of being crooked."

"My family wasn't happy about my decision to get into a relationship, but at that point I was grown, at least in terms of age. I didn't want to admit that I was sensing a trend with me and these men. I just told myself this was different. In a lot of ways he was different than what I was used to. I noticed, though, that in a lot of ways, he was the same."

"He wanted me to change too many things about myself. Wear dresses and skirts instead of pants. If it was cold, pants could go under dresses or skirts. He wanted me to wear my hair natural, not permed. Don't drink alcohol. In his defense, he thought he was helping me, improving me, and God knows I needed both."

"He thought he was doing what was best for me, but best by what definition and defined by who? The church you attend is not of the religion for us. There were so many things to get used to. He was quite the revolutionary man in words, thoughts, and deeds. We were used to being strong-willed and truthfully, his controlling nature didn't involve beating or intimidating me into submission, so it couldn't be that bad."

"We developed a different lifestyle, a holistic, afro-centric lifestyle. He was a hard man with good intentions. He wanted to practice a polygamous way of life. Although I'm no expert on the subject, I do know that in order for that lifestyle to be successful, certain systems must be put in place and certain criteria must be upheld. I also know that this was not an acceptable attempt by any means. I will give him credit where it is due. He ran our household like a business. He actually is a business owner. He was an entrepreneur whose business grew to the point that he opened an actual brick & mortar, which has now been in operation for over 20 years."

"Yes, it is an accomplishment for a small business. Both of our children have grown up there being actual employees. Ajamou has been back more than a couple of times as a full-time employee. Rashidah has also worked there a lot, especially during the summers and on weekends. Their father is now considered a village elder and is very respected in the community."

"Our first pregnancy was rough. There were several trips to the hospital for dehydration. That always had me on edge, not just because I was concerned for the baby, but after several years of being clean, I still wasn't comfortable with being poked with a needle and having it left in my arm."

"I knew right away that our first baby was a girl. I just felt it. It took about five years to conceive. I didn't blame their father for that, nor did I subscribe to the *everything happens when it's supposed to* theory. I blamed myself. Every month when I got my period, I'd cry. I had finally decided I wanted a baby and it seemed that the years of abuse to my body was preventing it from happening. I thought the drugs, sex, and the lifestyle in general had ruined my chances."

"Once I was able to confirm pregnancy, I prayed that my child would be born perfect and not suffer because of my past decisions. Every single day I prayed and hoped for the best while trying not to think about the worst. The relationship with our children's father was not what I wanted it to be, but deep inside me, I didn't believe I deserved what I wanted. I could have been okay with not having the happily ever after, but I could not be okay with something being wrong with my baby."

"My prayer was...*God please don't punish me for all the wrong I've done by taking my baby or not allowing her to be perfect. I know I've disappointed you, my family, and for what it's worth, even myself. But please, please don't take it out on my child. I promise that if you give me a healthy baby, I will spend my life becoming the virtuous woman you intended me to be.*"

"I know right? That was a long shot because all things considered, we were a train wreck. Our relationship with their father had its ups and downs. A lot of the time, the downs were up. It was hard because I rode on his good name. He was well-known and highly respected in the community. I, on the other hand, was new around here. I had no real reputation to stand on."

"For years, I felt like I walked in his shadow. He was sometimes a flawed man and other times he was a great man. I guess that could apply to all of us. We went through some good times and some not so good times. After the birth of our daughter, we separated. I took our baby and stayed with a friend. He, his mother, and my mother were all driving me crazy. Plus, I was suffering from post-partum depression. I was never diagnosed but I learned enough later to know that was exactly the case."

"I was also admitting to myself that even though I loved him, I was no longer in love, so I left. Yes, I went back, and we had our son. I was happy in my new role as a mommy but not in my home. So, I left again with two little ones. This time, I knew there'd be no going back. It was not an easy or pain-free separation by any means. I had limited resources and two babies, with no solid idea about what to do with either situation."

"Girl, hell yes, I struggled. It took some time, a lot of time before their dad and I could see eye to eye on anything. For most of their lives, I thought I needed his approval to see myself as a good mother. Oh, yes, we are good now. I would say we've gotten to a place where we are friends. There have been times where he's really shown genuine concern and care, and I can honestly say that if I need anything he is there. He has his granddaughter, who I also claim as mine. We are trying to raise her the best way we can, and we could not do it without each other."

"Striking out on my own was hard, though. For so long, I was so tired, so angry, so bitter, so done. At one point, I worked a full-time job and a part-time job. Other times, I would add a third, part-time job. It was more than rough. Most days I didn't know if I was coming or going. Everything I did was on autopilot. If it was just me, it wouldn't have been so bad, but I was responsible for two of the most precious beings born into this world, so I had to get it right."

"I felt like a loser when the relationship with their dad failed, even though I did all I could to make it work. I felt like a statistic again. We came from a home with divorced parents. We dropped out of high school. We got addicted to drugs. Now, we had two children outside of marriage and we were a single-parent household. Statistic, statistic, statistic."

"After their father, there were multiple relationships with men and even a couple of short-lived relationships with women. No, we are not a lesbian. I've always believed that it's hard to live in a box when it comes to who we are. The fact is, I used the word 'relationship' when it involved women, but it was really a friendship with benefits, at least that's an acceptable terminology in some circles."

"On the other hand, the men were sometimes drop-ins and other times live ins. Looking back Sis, we were most attracted to and ended up with men we thought we could fix. What? Why? I don't really know. Maybe we thought it would keep us from having to fix self or maybe we thought that helping others was necessary since life had helped us. Either way, I was still such a mess that I don't know what made me feel like I could fix anyone else."

"Did I love them? Well, I suppose I did. When I dissect the past, I've learned that there is a big difference between loving and being in love. You and I have loved men, no doubt, but as far as really being in love, I think that's only happened three times in our life. Two of them are now dead. The third, yes, he is still here but there will never be what I want when it comes to him. I'm not sorry for loving him but I regret falling in love with him."

"Affairs of the heart are not always easy to manage. I can proudly say that we've gotten better at it, though. I wanted so much to be what the world said we should be – a married mother with a successful life. We weren't legally married to our children's dad, though we were together for years."

"We ended up marrying a man we met through a friend, and we married him much too soon after that first meeting. The marriage didn't last. Our ex-husband was a recovering addict, who slid back down the rabbit hole of addiction after a while. He left, and I took him back. I wanted to be the perfect wife, to support the Black man who got treated so badly by life. Finally, after he lost his job and didn't tell us, cleaned out our bank account, and started making reckless decisions, I knew I had to take the kids and leave."

"So I did. I took what I could and moved into a place I couldn't afford. Because I took the first place that accepted me, we got evicted. I went to court, made arrangements I couldn't keep, and found another place. But it was too late, and we couldn't beat the clock. One morning, two days before I was scheduled to uproot my family again, the sheriff and some movers came to sit my stuff, my children's stuff, our entire life out on the curb. With nowhere to go for a couple of days, I watched the rain fall and soak everything I owned. It soaked me too which was okay because the rain created a camouflage for the tears that I could not hold back."

"I had no options. So, I called the children's father and he came to our rescue. He rented a truck to store our things until we could move into our new place, and he let us in for a couple of days. My level of embarrassment was heavy but not as heavy as my desire to see our children safe and our possessions secure. So I humbly welcomed the help. I swore, in that moment, that I'd never go through that again and thank God we haven't. For me, some things should only happen once, if at all, and being evicted is one of those things."

"Will I marry again? Ha, I say to that. Seriously though, I suppose we should never say never. But I don't see it in my future. It's not that I don't want a life partner, because I do have a desire for that. However, I don't have a potential mate. It's almost funny to hear myself say that, because I will fall for potential in a man quick. I don't know if it's my desire to fix them that attracts me, or my desire to help make their life better because mine has been made better."

"I used to think it was that I wanted to show my brothers that I believed in them even if the world didn't. I wanted to show that I felt sympathy for the plight of the Black man because life has done him so wrong. But you know Sis, I'm over that at this point. The truth is that life hasn't been peaches and cream for us as Black women either. I'm not going to get on a soapbox about it right now, even though I could."

"The bottom line is that for whatever the Black man has gone through, we've been there beside him supporting him, picking up the pieces and trying to glue them back together. My question has become who is gluing us back together? Who is holding me together when I'm falling apart?"

"What? No, I'm not in a relationship, although I do have a few feelings floating around out here. Sometimes I'm okay with that, and other times I'm not.

What I am becoming more okay with is putting myself, us and our need and wants higher on the ladder. We can't get everything our way, but we have to decide what is a deal breaker and what we are willing to accept. There is a difference between giving in to some things and giving up everything."

"Anyway, after the eviction, we got in a new place and we managed to rebuild. By this time, I was feeling like the queen of do-overs and rebuilding. Our babies grew and for the most part, I think they'd tell you that they had a good childhood. I see that makes you smile. Their lives were filled with school, friends, and activities. They often had friends over, sometimes for days or more at a time. Our home was the center of activity, even when my bed was in the living room. I knew where the children were most of the time, so I didn't mind. I guess it was part of our journey to becoming a village, which we are to this day."

"During our time in this Midwest melting pot, I've searched and searched for redemption, for our place in the world, for what I thought it was supposed to be, for us. We were raised Christian, Baptist to be exact. We attended a catholic school, studied Islam and ancient African religion, and wanted desperately in all of that to connect to a higher power. We didn't want a higher power we had to share. We wanted one that belonged only to us."

"Once the children were born, I searched and hoped I'd find what I was looking for by pouring myself into the children. They became everything to me, including my excuse for not dealing with self. You may or may not be surprised, Sis, to learn that I didn't live alone until we turned 49-years-old. We were either with a parent, a man, or the children. The only time we came close was when the preacher's kid was locked up. That didn't really count though because we knew he was coming back after his time as a guest with the state. I still used that place we called home to occasionally trick out of, so even with him gone, I wasn't really alone. Even when I was off the clock, sometimes they'd show up there."

"When it was time to move from the family dynamic with the children, I went to live and work on a local farm that was known for its work in the community gardens, worm farming, aquaponics, and an assortment of other things. Rashidah found her first apartment; it was a studio. I don't know if she knew how I cried privately, behind closed doors about that. Some of those tears were because she was striking out on her own, some of them were because so was I. Ajamou went to stay with their father for a while. I can't wait for you to get to know them. You will love them, not only because they are your children, but because of the people that they are."

"Forty-nine is also the year I was diagnosed with CHF – Cognitive Heart Failure. I knew something was wrong, but like a lot of Black women do, I kept putting on my superhero cape to save everyone in the world but myself. Since then, I've been hospitalized several times for the same thing; the doctors are now saying that without the surgery, my chances aren't good and one of these episodes could likely be my last. My God. Don't cry. I'm still here and you're here, too. I know it seems like we went through so much only to end up like that. Why us? Why not us?"

"Every time I go through this, it takes more out of me physically, mentally, and emotionally. It's also scary for our children. I looked it up once and found at that time that for Black women over twenty, 49% of them are affected with heart disease. Can you believe it? What are we allowing ourselves to deal with? What are we putting ourselves through? I'm rambling again."

"Once I started recovering from my initial diagnosis, I had to learn to accept my condition. It made me want to go on a quest to find the meaning for my life, for our life. I felt like I'd been on that journey for years, but for some reason it was different now."

"You think so? Yes, maybe one day you and I will write a book. Together we have one hell of a story. We learned a lot together and I've learned even more than that. I want to share with you and anyone who will listen. We make it harder than it has to be. I've looked for purpose and answers in geographical changes, children, countless relationships, church, almost any and everything, Sis. I've looked."

"I think I made it harder than it needed to be. I think many of us make it harder than it has to be. I slowly came to the realization that I had to face my past in order to understand my present and my purpose. I had to face you in order to deal with me. I had to look into your eyes with my eyes and say some things out loud, not in a hushed whisper. I had to almost yell at them to frighten away the demons that have been trying to reside in my life."

"I had to look at things from another perspective to truly see how blessed we are. We started having reckless, unprotected sex way too young but haven't contracted any disease that killed us. We worked in the sex industry, that didn't kill us. We dropped out of high school and gave up two opportunities to go to college, but we are one of the wisest women I know. We lost a child and aborted another, but we gave birth to and raised two of the dopest people on the planet, and have taken many more in as ours to love and nurture."

"We had a drug habit that cost hundreds of dollars per day and the skill that we developed with a needle because of it helped us give our son the injections he needed during his treatment and recovery. We suffer with heart disease and a weak heart, but we still have the capacity to give love beyond measure and we have one of the biggest hearts."

"We've been harmed by touch, beaten by hands, yet we know how to hold on to people and hug them as if their prayers are being answered. We didn't make it with our children's father. For whatever reason, we weren't meant to stay together for life. However, in him I have a protector, an advocate, and a friend. I know people who've been married for 20 years that can't say that."

"Today, I had to face you, naked and vulnerable in my truth. I had to come to you like a woman to apologize and admit that we are better together than apart. I got sick and tired of being sick and tired. I grew weary of using my strength to hold the closet door closed to stop the skeletons from falling out into a pile of lies, judgment, guilt, safe hatred or anything else they might reveal. I had to know that I was okay with me so that I could offer you something better than what we had. I felt responsible, beloved, and I could not take you on another journey that wouldn't end well."

"So, you see, I had to get it right for your sake, our sake, our children's sake. I had to begin to face the fear of not enough. The fear of not doing enough, not being enough, not knowing enough. I had to say I've had enough of not enough. Oh no, Sis, I never thought of you as a burden or dead weight. I just thought if I left you there, I could stop you from being hurt more than you already had been."

"So, I struck out on a life that was foreign and unsure. I went on a hunt and needed to come back with something other than an apology to fill your spiritual belly. I had given that to myself a million times and there was no satisfaction in that without real work, without a perspective change. Maybe I was wrong to leave you behind. Maybe I should have come back sooner, despite how I felt. Maybe the fact that I'm a control freak made me want to orchestrate the type of life I thought we deserved."

"Either way, I can't do anything about it now. The past is the past and I'm glad you're not in the past anymore. I just couldn't face you with the way things were. Shit, I could barely face myself and that took the better part of three decades. I just hope, as I've said before, that you can forgive me and find it in your heart to understand."

"I know you have a million questions and I want to answer every single one, and the ones that come after that. Okay, go ahead and ask a couple, if you'd like. Good question. Do I miss getting high? Well, for years I did. I still cringe if there is a movie scene and people are cooking or shooting dope. Truthfully, sometimes I turn my head or close my eyes. I don't miss it anymore. Every once in a while, I will have a dream using. That tells me I need to get something off my mind or in order in my life."

"Regrets? Wow, I don't have many because everything makes us who we are, and today I know we're not what we used to be. As we strive to be better, we are enough as we are. My biggest regret is probably all the years I wasted trying to figure out life without you, not coming back for you right away. That is wasted time that neither of us can get back."

"Am I happy? That is a tough question, because we all define happiness differently and I think that definition changes as our life changes. I will say I'm more content than I've ever been. I'm more hopeful than I've ever been, and I'm taking more responsibility for my life, our life, than I ever have. That makes me happy. I know what it is to love and be loved. That makes me happy. I can also say that life is not fireworks and smiley faces all the time. I'm okay with that, too, because I've found out that I can shift that, maybe not in the world, but in our world."

"What is more important than being happy is being grateful. That in itself is a form of happiness. I want you to find your place of happiness. I want you to know that your wounds, internal and external, are not ugly. They are medals that you earned as a survivor. I want you to walk on your shaky legs, unstable from decades of no use, knowing that you have me and a support system of strong women who will support you and hold you up. I want you and I to be examples to our sisters, our daughters, and their reflections."

"I know it's been a lot and I'll follow your cue. When you want to talk more, we will. Yes, you have another question. What is the greatest lesson I've learned? Child, that question has multiple answers because all lessons are great. The one that comes to mind right away is that my life is my life and in order to be okay with it, I must accept it. I can't pick it apart and only accept what I want. It doesn't mean that I can't have some things go a certain way or even that I have to like them. It means that if I can accept and own the total package of who and what I've been, then I can accept and own who, and what I am."

"If you don't want to ask more questions, but just want to talk, I'm here to listen. I understand. It's been a lot. Do you mind if I hold your hand? We can walk to the porch and sit in unspoken conversation remembering our past, living our present, and preparing for our future. I won't run anymore, and I won't chase things unnamed. I am moving forward when it comes to our life, you have my word. I'll share my fears, my thoughts, my struggles, my dreams and my hopes with you. I've finally learned my life will be easier if I reflect with my reflection."

"This book is jaw dropping and really puts the reader in the life of the writer. Clara Fleming gives her reflection of herself to understand herself while learning the meaning of life and living for herself. It's a must read..." **Author/Publisher Kendrick Watkins**

Coming soon by Clara Fleming

'Generational Orgasms'

Follow her at:
Website: Clarafleming.com
Facebook: Clara Fleming
Email: claraifleming@gmail.com